# Identity
# Politics of
# Difference

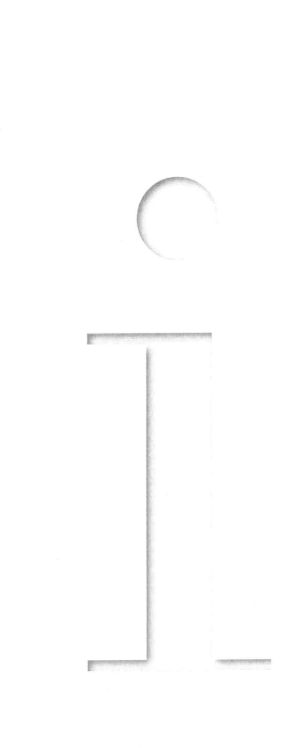

# Identity Politics of Difference

## THE MIXED-RACE AMERICAN INDIAN EXPERIENCE

Michelle R. Montgomery

UNIVERSITY PRESS OF COLORADO
*Louisville*

© 2017 by University Press of Colorado

Published by University Press of Colorado
245 Century Circle, Suite 202
Louisville, Colorado 80027

 The University Press of Colorado is a proud member of
ASSOCIATION of UNIVERSITY PRESSES   the Association of University Presses.

The University Press of Colorado is a cooperative publishing enterprise supported, in part,
by Adams State University, Colorado State University, Fort Lewis College, Metropolitan State
University of Denver, Regis University, University of Colorado, University of Northern Colorado,
Utah State University, and Western State Colorado University.

∞ This paper meets the requirements of the ANSI / NISO Z39.48–1992 (Permanence of Paper).

ISBN: 978-1-60732-543-7 (cloth)
ISBN: 978-1-64642-190-9 (paperback)
ISBN: 978-1-60732-544-4 (ebook)

Library of Congress Cataloging-in-Publication Data

Names: Montgomery, Michelle R., author.
Title: Identity politics of difference : the mixed-race American Indian experience / Michelle R.
    Montgomery.
Description: Boulder : University Press of Colorado, [2017] | Includes bibliographical references
    and index.
Identifiers: LCCN 2016035720 | ISBN 9781607325437 (cloth) | ISBN 9781646421909 (pbk) | ISBN
    9781607325444 (ebook)
Subjects: LCSH: Indian college students—Ethnic identity. | Indians of North America—Education
    (Higher) | Indian college students—Attitudes. | Academic achievement. | Racially mixed peo-
    ple—Race identity—United States. | Identity politics.
Classification: LCC E96 .M66 2017 | DDC 378.1/ 982997—dc23
LC record available at https:/ / lccn.loc.gov / 2016035720

# Contents

# Acknowledgments

Throughout my graduate school career at the University of New Mexico and the University of Washington, I was lucky to have some great mentors. Ricky Lee Allen, Kelly Edwards, Polly Olsen, and Daniel Wildcat provided crucial support. My grandfather James O. Baker was an early hero of mine. I learned from him that a life lived well with integrity is not always easy. He taught me to care less about things that don't matter and to be more strategic in pursuing things that do. A true friend and mentor, Tim Bennett has regularly reminded me not to settle for less than I deserve and encouraged me to be more ambitious in my expectations. Thanks as well to the University Press of Colorado. Finally, this book honors the participants who shared their lived experiences with me.

# PART I
# THE POLITICS OF MULTIRACIALISM

# 1

# History of Racial Hierarchy and Race "Mixture"

Racial identifications are not individual markers but are developed in relation to collective identities within racialized societies and spaces, products of historical, political, and social struggles. This is particularly true within learning environments—something happens in schools, especially regarding how racial identities are formed and assigned in ways that affect schooling experiences.

I have brown skin and wavy hair. In my experiences as a student and teacher, I became accustomed to being asked, "What are you?" Often I am mistaken for being reserved despite my easy, sincere grin. My facial expression perhaps does not show what I have learned in my life: reluctant people endure; passionate people live. Whether it is the glint of happiness in my eyes or what I call using laughter to heal your soul, my past experience as a mixed-race person has been significantly different from my current outlook on life. I am at ease with my lived experiences, very willing to share, and I even encourage others to probe more deeply into my racialized experiences. Like many mixed-race people, I experienced an epiphany: disowning a need

DOI: 10.5876/9781607325444.c001

to belong, disengaging from the structure of race has given me the confidence to critique race discourse and racialized spaces.

I identify as American Indian with mixed-race heritage. I am mixed-race black/white,[1] American Indian, and mixed-race Korean/Mongolian. My father is mixed-race black/white and American Indian, and my mother is mixed-race Korean/Mongolian. We are enrolled members of the Haliwa Saponi Tribe and descendants of the Eastern Band Cherokee Tribe. When I was growing up, my father taught me that I am a multiracial person, a descendant of two tribes, and American Indian.[2] Unfortunately, a person cannot be enrolled in more than one tribe. So, I can personally relate to the idea that monoraciality does not fit my multiracial and tribal identities or those of other multiracials in our so-called melting pot society.

However, countless numbers of times I have been raced in ways that have forced me to choose a group association. My own experiences illustrate how racial designation and group association play out in society, including in classroom learning environments. My siblings and I grew up in northeastern North Carolina in an American Indian community that also included mixed-race American Indians with black, American Indian, and white ancestry.[3] I attended a rural high school that contained mixed-race American Indians, monoracial blacks, monoracial American Indians, and monoracial white students. It was not unusual for mixed-race black/American Indian and monoracial blacks to create close group associations, which were exhibited through social interactions that occurred when sitting together in the cafeteria, classrooms, or in designated lounging areas around campus. However, mixed-race white/American Indian students, especially those who seemed phenotypically white, did not want to be associated with monoracial black students. Most mixed-race white/American Indian students chose to create group associations with monoracial white students. As a brown-complexioned multiracial person who identified as American Indian in this racially polarized environment, I was placed in a situation where I had to choose a group association to keep mixed-race black/American Indian and monoracial black students from viewing me as acting white. On the other hand, the mixed-raced white/American Indians and monoracial whites viewed my actions as acting black.

Because of my Korean and Mongolian ancestry, I was not perceived phenotypically as a true member of the black or American Indian groups. My Korean and Mongolian aspects caused friction with the monoracial black and mixed-race black/American Indian groups with which I most commonly associated because it gave me an inroad to the white (or whiter) groups that they did not have. Because I did not acknowledge or challenge my advantage, I allowed myself to be used as an agent of racism. This happened in a number of ways. For instance, monoracial white and mixed-race American Indian groups asked me to sit with them in the cafeteria, but they did not invite monoracial blacks and mixed-race black/American Indians. And I accepted their invitation. As a consequence, the group with which I most associated viewed me as a race traitor, as a racial fraud. And I felt like one, too. I am ashamed that I actively participated in the disparagement of blacks, which is the most denigrated part of my own ancestry. A multiracial person with black ancestry who accepts not being identified as black in an effort to subvert white privilege (i.e., resisting racial categorization as a way of challenging the notion of race) can actually be reinforcing it, as was the case for me. The problem is how the context and meaning of being a race traitor or committing racial fraud arise out of and are bounded by the social and political descriptions of race. Both social and political constructs are then used as a justification for policing the accuracy of racial identification or political alliance. In most instances, being cast as a race traitor, or as an alleged racial fraud, is a constitutive feature of the dynamics of the informal school setting and is further developed in the formal schooling setting of the learning environment.[4] In other words, the daily routines of schools actively construct the racial hierarchy of the United States, with multiracial students playing a key role.

Since racial identity is a social and political construct, it acquires meaning in the context of a particular set of social relationships. In a tribal college setting, the identity politics of blood quantum often influences the multiracial experience of students (i.e., being an enrolled member of a state or federally recognized tribe, and recognized as a descendant based on phenotypic features). Allen (2006) explains, "As a social institution, public schooling should be understood as a site where the reproduction of (and resistance to) the white supremacist totality is played out" (10). The mixed-race student's choice of a racial identity in both an informal and formal learning environment is made for practical purposes. As such, students' racial identity choices are based on how they perceive themselves or how they wish others to perceive them.

The identity choice of multiracial students is shaped by the dominant culture of society. Their identity choices are far from being open and free. Rather, as evidenced through my life experience, these choices are constrained by the structural organization of the racialized social system. This contradicts "commonsense" notions of multiracial identity, including the idea that multiracial people can freely pick and choose from their various racial ancestries to construct a nondeterministic self-representation. The evidence for using a structural approach to thinking about multiraciality exists everywhere. For example, it is common knowledge that home situations, school environments, and images from the mass media strongly influence our youth. Unfortunately, the negative stereotypes and poor treatment of blacks and others deemed blackened often influence identity choice for multiracials because they see that there is an advantage to being identified as nonblack. In addition, the curriculum of public schools is structured to cast white or lighter-skinned people as superior and darker-skinned people as inferior.

For this reason, a New Mexico tribal college provided a rich environment for my study of racial identity. In this setting, Spanish/white identity was an option for lighter-skinned mixed-race people, but darker-skinned persons were forced into a Mexican/mestiza/o identity. These dynamics influenced "Indianness."[5] Since the traditional identity of New Mexican people has been understood as mixed raced (Spanish and American Indian ancestry), it was important to examine how heritage, self-perceptions, and social institutions construct the making of Indianness. The role of heritage in a student's sense of identity in learning environments is affected by both overt and hidden school curricula as well as by macro and micro social processes.

My research was a continuation of efforts to understand my personal experiences with my own multiracial American Indian identity. The key difference between my research and my personal quest for understanding was that instead of unveiling answers to my personal questions about schooling experiences, I was seeking ways to help multiracial students understand and interpret how schools, society, and communities influence the identities of mixed-race people. My positioning in this research was as a multiracial American Indian scholar and educator. As a scholar, I was interested in researching identity as a quasi-selective choice in which one is not only raced *but also acts racially*. In other words, mixed-race students are not simply passive victims of racial categorization; they are active agents who have the option to conform to or resist the racial order. So, while the racial situation of mixed-race students is highly structural, there still exists some element of choice, or agency, which can be expressed in the way that mixed-race students see themselves in relation to other raced groups. As an educator, I was interested in how mixed-race students at a tribal college that focuses on the contemporary and traditional expressions of American Indian/Indigenous people understand their racial identity choices and how political institutions assist multiracial students through their racialized schooling experiences. It is important for educators to understand the ways their actions can contribute to how schools often reinforce and reproduce inequality and power differences (Alfred 2004; Allen 2006; Mihesuah 2004). To meet these goals, my research offers experiential information situated within a theoretical framework that scholars and educators can use to think critically about multiraciality in classrooms.

## Researching the Role of Schools and Mixed-Race Identity Choices

The rate of interracial marriages has increased drastically over the last few decades: by almost 300 percent since 1970 (Cruz 2001; Williams 2006). Although the mixed-raced population is growing and multiracialism is fast becoming a popular racial issue (Rockquemore and Brunsma 2002), the overall percentage of the total population that identifies as multiracial remains low. The 2000 US census found that only 2.4 percent of the population identified as multiracial (US Census Bureau 2000). Nevertheless, that percentage is approximately 7 million people, a population larger than that of most major US cities. Nearly half are under age twenty-five, suggesting that this percentage will rise as the current population ages ("Multiracials: Population" 2002).

Through an inescapable web of images and language, society labels multiracial students to the point that they come to internalize and use these labels themselves. Racial categorization operates at the level of perception. We learn to "see" race and assign people into racial groups. Multiracial people are sized up, or "racially measured," as people try to decipher where they fit within the existing racial categories and hierarchy.[6] "What are you?" is a question most multiracial people have been asked.

However, not all multiracials experience racial measurement in the same way. For example, a dark or brown mixed-race person of black heritage is more often racially measured as being monoracial (i.e., "just black") than "other" or lighter-skinned mixed-race people. This is in large part the legacy of the one drop rule that existed during slavery. Despite a person with black phenotypic features identifying as mixed race, racial measures have historically read black heritage as fixed and clear-cut, making a rather multiracial group (US blacks) appear largely monoracial. Even within groups, such as with Latinos, black Latinos experience a lower social status than do those of lighter skin color and/or different heritages. This anti-blackness, which sees black as being inferior and less desirable than nonblack, pervades much of the political discourse surrounding multiracialism. For example, President Barack Obama is biracial (the son of a black Kenyan father and a white US mother). Yet, the media monoracially labels him as black. Seemingly aware of how multiracial politics can detract from the situations of all racial groups, President Obama has stated that mixed-race people ought to "avoid focusing so narrowly on their own experiences that they become detached from larger struggles of racism and inequality" (DaCosta 2007, 182).

Since any label other than white relegates them to a lower status, it is not surprising that many multiracial students feel pressured to choose an identity with a higher status in order to feel socially and personally accepted. However, some resist the temptation to identify as close to white as possible and instead choose to identify with the most oppressed side of their racial ancestry. Such is the case with many multiracial individuals with black heritage who refer to themselves as "black" as opposed to "multiracial." To them, embracing a black identity is an important vehicle for self-empowerment, whereas multiracial suggests a type of identity maneuver to gain heightened status. In other words, the "choice" of a racial identity is also a political choice for mixed-race people. They can choose between complicity with or resistance against the larger white supremacist structure that offers more privilege to those seen as less dark.

Since the actions of multiracials have important consequences for their own and other groups, approaches to multiracialism are inherently political, not merely a matter of personal preference. Multiracialism is political because there are competing racial agendas representing different ideological camps, all of them fighting to have their agenda shape normative thinking on multiracialism and, by extension, race and racism. However, current every-day thinking on multiracialism does not seem to grasp the fuller meaning of multiracial politics as it manifests itself in a hierarchical racial system like that in the United States. In other words, the politics of multiracialism affects not only those who are multiracial but also everyone else.

The continuation of racial segregation within society among mixed-race people will depend on how they perceive themselves in relation to others. This becomes problematic as groups attempt to be "a little less black and therefore a little less subordinate" (Makalani 2001, 84). Not all folks have this kind of choice; some cannot pass as anything but black. But, in a different context, these experiences create a platform for examining the ways mixed-race students resist or actively participate in maintaining structured racial hierarchies. The outcome is mixed-race students acting as agents to reinforce racial hierarchies. Also, the lived aspect of racial identity choice in schools creates shifting contexts for measuring and/or understanding the effects of such experiences.

Schools provide an important environment since they have typically addressed the importance of race—if they address it at all—from a monora-cial perspective. For example, schools use racial information about their students to track achievement. The problem arises when schools racially measure mixed-race students and assign them into a monolithic multiracial typology, as if students' differences in skin tone and phenotype do not mat-ter. In our alleged "color-blind" era, paying attention to the realities of the color line would be frowned upon, even deemed "racist." The color-blind ideological approach proclaims that we should not notice differences among multiracial people. Yet, in the everyday realities of race, whites tend to be more accepting of those who appear whiter. The result is a racial hierarchy that ranges from light to dark and corresponds to material outcomes. Blumer (1958) and Bonilla-Silva (1996) explain that racial hierarchy is premised on the notion that race is a material symbol (i.e., light-skinned multiracials position-ing themselves within a racial hierarchy above darker-skinned multiracials) based on the conception of one's own racial group defined by the preju-diced images and conceptions of the dominant racial group and positioned in relation to other racial groups. To further explain this point, "One should keep clearly in mind that people necessarily come to identify themselves as belonging to a racial group [e.g., a mixed-race group]; such identification is not spontaneous or inevitable but a result of experience" (Blumer 1958, 3). And, by assisting in the construction of a middle buffer group (light- or medium-skinned multiracials) above a lower-status racialized group (blacks and darker-skinned Latinos) (Bonilla-Silva 2003), schools provide a competitive environment for students to either avoid being labeled racially or to choose a racial label that best matches their desired personal interests.

In addition to providing students with meaningful educational opportunities, schools also serve as entities where identities are cultivated and enacted (Lewis 2005; Lopez 2003; Mihesuah 2004). This study examines how schools influence the identity choices of mixed-race students. In addition, it explores the ways in which students represent their identity choices and lived experiences through the lens of a racialized social hierarchy.

## The Process of Discovery

Due to the heightened popularity of multiracial issues, it was important in my study to think beyond the current politically naive discourse on multiracials and consider how these individuals will not only resist racism but also redefine racial hierarchies. I wanted to study the racial identity choices and lived experiences of mixed-race students with American Indian heritage who attended a tribal college in New Mexico to help contextualize students' representations of their racial identity choices in light of the influences of societal and community factors. In other words, I wanted to explore beyond a dehumanizing multiracial-as-victim approach and instead see students as active racial agents who could conform to and/or resist a racist system based upon a complex racial hierarchy. There is a lack of educational literature representing mixed-race individuals, especially those of mixed race with American Indian heritage, as people who use their choice of identity politically and socially to their own individual advantage. Also, it is important to explore where phenotypically black mixed-race people fit into racial identity classification schemes. Using a combination of interviews and group sessions, I examined the ways in which college students identified their race and how that identity changed over time or across context. This was accomplished by getting to know students' beliefs, biographies, and significant racial events in their lives, especially those events that occurred within the confines of institutions.

In addition, there is limited literature on race issues in tribal colleges, in particular on how to educate students, administrators, and educators regarding mixed-race students. Data is absent on how institutions influence the beliefs and social views of mixed-race students. For students of mixed descent, questions of blood quantum and stereotypical notions of American Indian phenotypes or surnames are compounded by how mixed-race Indianness is defined (Cramer 2005; Garroutte 2003; Mihesuah 2004). Also, skin color—and the experience of a particular skin color—plays a major role in determining membership in school peer groups (Tatum 1997). Another problem is that if there are no antiracist administrators, educators, or student learning objectives within a school, then mixed-race students are left to figure out the answers themselves. Often the result is an intensely negative set of race relations that goes unexamined. Since the significant distinctions of race and phenotype are socially constructed and subjected to social measures, it is thus important for institutions, administrators, and educators to acknowledge their definitions of racial identity in daily schooling interaction. When these definitions are negative and harmful, they reinforce the context of group membership status (inferior or superior intellect, behaviors, perception of oneself, etc.).

Another issue is the lack of research conducted on the influence of socially practiced racial classification schemes on the experiences of mixed-race students' identity choice. Although I have taught a number of mixed-race students, it was my own experience as a multiracial educator who identifies as American Indian living in New Mexico that guided me to analyze mixed-race issues in learning environments. In addition, as I had done as a high school student, a number of the mixed-race students I taught in New Mexico had acculturated to the dominant ideology of a racial hierarchy that denigrated blacks as the most inferior race. I began to wonder why administrators and other educators had not been trained to recognize the issues of mixed-race students, not to mention the problem of a predominant racial ideology that supports a hierarchical arrangement of various racial groups. To address the issues outlined above, I conducted research to see if this pattern persists in a tribal college in the same region. It was also an opportunity to intervene in this problematic view of race.

This research challenges us to think about what it means to identify as mixed race while paying attention to historical and contextual influences. It also forces us to address which mixed-race individuals are always cast into monoracial identities, which others expand the borders of whiteness, and which are given a waiting status or serve as a buffer group into white membership (Bonilla-Silva 2003).

The findings of this study will contribute to an understanding of the racial identity influences on mixed-race college students with American Indian heritage in both formal and informal school settings. This information will assist with decolonizing curricula to become antiracist and developing critically needed teacher education programs. Also, it is intended to provide future educators with a theoretical connection between the influence of the US racial hierarchy in school settings and the creation of conflictual environments that shape the identity choices of mixed-race students. Also, the expectations of this study are to assist multiracial students in understanding the consequences of their identity choices, beliefs, and actions for members of other racial groups and the role schools and society play in racial identity formation.

Grounded in the premise that racial identity choice is an individual enactment with structural implications, this study sought to explore the formal and informal schooling experiences that influence the racial identity choices of mixed-race college students. Therefore, the research questions addressed in this study are as follows: How do the formal and informal schooling contexts shape the identity choices of multiracial students? How do the identity choices of multiracial students conform to and/or resist the racialized social system of the United States?

## Notes

1. The term *black* is purposely used instead of *African American* to depict the historical notions of a racial classification scheme.

2. I will alternate between the terms *multiracial* and *mixed-race* depending on the situation I am explaining or describing. I will use *mixed-race* more often because the students I interviewed use *mixed* to refer to their racial identities.

3. The term *white* is used instead of *Anglo* or *European* because it is race-focused and commonly used by the students I interviewed.

4. An informal school setting is comprised of the social aspects of relationships and peer influences. A formal school setting refers to the curriculum, administrators, policies, educators, and power structures, and the means by which they affect the identity choices of mixed-race students.

5. Regarding Indianness, it should be noted that "looking Indian" can be of greater importance than one's biological or legal status.

6. For example, the mixed-race perspective in this study raises questions about how race is measured in society as a lived experience. Through a historical formation of race, decisions are made about a person based on phenotypic attributes as a racial measure. As a result, mixed-race people are conveniently racially categorized, which in turn often influences or shapes expectations and behaviors of them as racially measured people.

# 2

# Overview of Literature on Mixed-Race/Multiracial Students

There is little empirical research examining how schools influence the racial identity choices of multiracial students, in particular mixed-race students who identify as American Indian. Even more troubling is the lack of literature on the experiences of mixed-race students using racial identity choice as a social and political tool to negotiate race discourse, actions, and spaces. Therefore, piecing together a concise and appropriate literature review is a challenge. Nevertheless, my aim is to argue the need to look at the relationship between the racial agency of multiracial students and the larger white supremacist social structure. In order to present a broad view of the social and schooling contexts in which mixed-race people operate as active agents of racial classification schemes, this literature review will focus on two areas: (1) the politics of multiracialism, and (2) empirical research on the identity politics of multiracial students. Although I have studied one or more mixed-race categories in my data collection, this literature review focuses primarily on black, American Indian, Hispanic, and white mixedness.

DOI: 10.5876/9781607325444.c002

In looking at current research on multiracials in the United States, it is necessary to understand the debate over the creation of a "multiracial" group. The two main factions are those in favor of a government-recognized multiracial category, the "advocates," and those who are opposed to it, the "refuters" (Spencer 2006a). The key point of disagreement between advocates and refuters lies in the way each camp interprets the meaning and purpose of racial classification. Advocates cast racial classification in individualist terms. They argue that a multiracial category is an identity choice selected from among a variety of racial category options that should be available to individual mixed-race people (DaCosta 2007). Spencer (2006a) explains that "the 'advocates' of multiracial identity choice tend to operate from the assumption, necessitated by its fundamental position (whether admitted or not), that biological race exists as a physical reality" (2). Therefore, the advocates assume that individual mixed-race people need a multiracial category that reflects their biological reality. Conversely, the refuters criticize the biological constructs of race, arguing that race is a social and political construct. Refuters oppose a multiracial category also because they believe it takes political strength away from existing races, such as blacks. They believe that multiracials should choose an existing monoracial category.

The most contentious argument dividing the advocates and refuters is based on the situatedness of a multiracial category within the fact that race is a social process. Omi and Winant's 1994 *Racial Formation in the United States from the 1960s to the 1990s* argued that racial formation occurs at both macro and micro levels. Omi and Winant (1986) note, "The meaning of race is defined and contested throughout society, in both collective action and personal practice. In this process, racial categories themselves are formed, transformed, destroyed, and reformed . . . Racial formation . . . is the process by which social, economic and political forces determine the content of importance of racial categories, and by which they are in turn shaped by racial meanings. Crucial to this formulation is the treatment of race as a central axis of social relations, which cannot be subsumed under or reduced to some broader category or conception" (61–62).

Race, then, can be explained as a macro-level social process that is constructed as a collective body focused on the formation of structural sites of contestation, such as economic, political, and ideological (Omi and Winant 1986). Thus, a macro level of larger social forces and political projects influences the racial identity choices of multiracials. At the micro level, the individual identity choice of multiracials can be seen as an individual act of race being used for reasons of self-interest or social and political gain (Omi and Winant 1994). The macro forces operate beyond the micro individual racial identity choice. Currently, the macro forces that are supporting the use of a multiracial category fail to acknowledge the hierarchical system that is in place. The push for a multiracial category must then be seen as a kind of political project in which attention is being diverted from the real issue of racial hierarchy and the interests of whites are being concealed. Therefore, the discourse surrounding multiracial politics must be examined to see how multiracials are being positioned relative to other groups within the racialized US social system.

To critically analyze the debate, we must see the arguments of advocates and refuters through the lens of whose group or individual interests are being assisted or disenfranchised. Who are the stakeholders of each camp and what is their racial agenda? What does each have to gain relative to other racial groups? A common denominator in the majority of these discussions is that both sides ignore how mixed-race politics create divisions among three key groups: blacks who do not see themselves as mixed, blacks who claim a mixed identity, and people who claim a nonwhite mixed identity. Nonetheless, the macro societal and political influences of race create an atmosphere in which a multiracial category does not challenge the overarching racialized social system. For example, the opportunity to choose distinct, more complex identities through support of a multiracial category can create further disenfranchisement for certain race groups; the rules change and along with them so will the racial politics. However, it is important to note that a multiracial category will give certain multiracials a tool to navigate pro-white realms if they align themselves with whiteness.

In examining the factors that influence racial identity choice among mixed-race people, a critical lens is important for questioning the power dynamics at play. Through the use of a Critical Race Theory (CRT) lens, one may see how race can be both asserted and assigned. CRT helps to reveal how white supremacy scripts the participation of mixed-race people in both ascribed and asserted racial identifications. It also provides a guide for defining a new discourse for mixed-race people.

According to Allen (2006), CRT explores more deeply the nature of white supremacy. Questioning the reality of whiteness brings to light exactly how and why certain mixed-race individuals are or are not recognized as mixed race. It pinpoints the source of their status within a racial hierarchy. "CRT challenges the ways in which notions such as objectivity, neutrality, meritocracy, and color blindness are used to construct White supremacy" (11).

Since there has been a surge of interest in mixed-race identity choice, it is important to consider if this emerging attention will create space for dialogue on issues of historical processes. For example, the Comanche captivity of girls and women created the historical formation of New Mexican mestizas/os or Mexicanness (of mixed-race Spanish and American Indian ancestry), which served as an identity counterpart to "Spanish American" identity development in New Mexico. Consequently, this new Spanish American identity was the byproduct of white racism targeting American Indians and Mexicans. The outcome was an identity that contextually positioned those who could identify as Spanish American, and thus as more purely European, in a higher group status. The Comanches' captivity of Spanish/American Indian females in the Southwest "helped to produce and spread influential ideas about 'Mexicanness' that tended to transform older colonial hierarchies of Spaniards and Indians in New Mexico" (Marez 2001, 271). The most immediate consequence of Spanish American identity was an increase in racial division. A non-Mexicanness or American Indian identity coincided with escalating levels of racial inequality alongside a slightly altered form of Spanish American white supremacy. Nieto-Phillips (2004) states, "The making of Spanish American identity offers a sometimes discomforting glimpse into the making of whiteness" (11).

When considering the dialectical relationship between Mexicans/mestizas/os and Spanish Americans in New Mexico, the following account by Nieto-Phillips (2004) is instructive: "The initial 'contaminant' of Spanish blood in America was 'Indian' blood: however, with the spread of African slavery, so-called negros (Blacks) also became an additional referent against which Spanish identity would be cast. Like Indians, African slaves were diverse in origin and culture, yet, in Spanish eyes, they too were seen as a singular, inferior people. The objectified Indian and African represented the antithesis to Spanish spiritual, racial, and cultural identity" (23).

This perspective of certain mixed-race unions and their status within a racial hierarchy is embedded within the existing rankings and inequalities of a white supremacist racial order. Allen (2006) explains, "Various race discourses totally miss the ideological and material dimensions of White supremacy" (12). And the inability of advocates of a mixed-race identity choice to see the permanent imbalances of power blinds them to the reality of how the social distance between mixed-race people and whites is also a function of the social distance between all racial groups. After all, white supremacy "determines relations of power, the re/production of labor divisions and property, the construction of social status, and the context and script of race struggles" (10).

Contrary to the beliefs of many advocates, a multiracial category neither stops white people from being blind to the realities of race nor challenges them to see themselves in explicitly racial terms. Although white people may not want to acknowledge individual and institutional white privilege, whiteness is linked to the reasons why various people of color will use a multiracial category to gain access to white identities and white privilege by identifying with a racial group, that is, multiracials, who are seen as being closer to white. In other words, my argument is that a multiracial category reinforces rather than challenges whiteness. To explain my assertion, I will focus on four main points: (1) the substitution of one race essentialism for another, (2) a color-blind multiracial agenda, (3) expanding the boundaries of whiteness, and (4) the resurrection of racial classification.

First, advocates' support of a multiracial category ultimately embraces the substitution of one race essentialist notion for another (Spencer 2006a). In other words, "multiracial" paradoxically becomes just one more monoracial category in a classification scheme designed around monoraciality. Also, multiracial would be (is) assigned a higher status than black and gives multiracials with black ancestry the possibility to be something other than black. The result is that it "reinscribes and reproduces Blackness in an essentialized and overtly biological way" (Spencer 2006b, 85). The advocate perspective fails to use a political focus on cross-racial alliances to dismantle the social formation of race, assuming naively that the multiracial category will disrupt the whole notion of classification and thus racism itself. In the process, it only reinforces the existing racial hierarchy by adding one more rung to the middle of the ladder. For example, Delpit (1995) asserts, "If you are not already a participant in the culture of power, being told explicitly the rules of that culture makes acquiring power easier" (25). The advocates of a multiracial category clearly believe that whiteness is attainable through the biological aspects of phenotype and skin tone and the cultural aspects of assimilating to whiteness. This requires an understanding to some extent of the white cultural ways of being. It requires cultural capital (Bourdieu 1986), which corresponds to the positionality of whites in the larger racial order. The advocacy for a multiracial category creates insider versus outsider positionalities vis-à-vis the white culture of power.

The reality is that issues of race cannot easily be separated from issues of power that have been historically embedded in society. For example, if advocacy for a multiracial category is blind to the operations of the culture of power, that creates discrimination effects for blacks and those of black heritage. As such, I would argue that those who advocate for a multiracial category are, consciously or not, oppressing others. Furthermore, Spencer (1997) accuses advocates of trying to create a three-tiered racial hierarchy (Allen 2005; Bonilla-Silva 2005) similar to the one in South Africa: whites on top, multiracials in the middle, and blacks on the bottom. Spencer (1999) asserts, "The challenge for America lies in determining how to move away from the fallacy of race while remaining aggressive in the battle against racism" (167). Adding another category will do little to change the problematic relations between racial groups.

One of the more intriguing aspects of the advocates' position is how they claim to be challenging race essentialism while at the same time reinforcing it. Race essentialism manifests itself in the attempt to define race by physical differences. Race essentialism is used as a mechanism of social division and racial stratification. The term *race,* in this view, refers solely to a group of people who have in common some visible physical traits, such as skin color, hair texture, facial features, and eye shape (Cramer 2005; Garroutte 2003; Hunter 2005; Lee 2005; Lewis 2005; Lopez 2003). As a result, such distinct phenotypic features are associated with racial membership. One's membership in a race is questioned if one does not possess these "essential" physical traits. Race essentialism, from a biological race perspective, places people into fixed, seemingly natural racialized categories.

Consequently, phenotypic features are symbols of race identity and status, whether we like it or not, because social interactions are shaped through the lens of biological race. Seeing race this way also plays into assigning differential human value to members of different racial groups, thus reinforcing the white supremacist belief in the inherent inferiority of people of color. Such beliefs eventually became institutionalized, reinforcing and reproducing systems of social inequality and status differences. For example, race essentialism was employed to create an inferior social status for people of African or black ancestry, which was reinforced and perpetuated through social mechanisms worldwide. In the United States, one of these social mechanisms was social Darwinism (Snipp 2002). From a racial perspective, social Darwinism was the idea that white nations had to civilize the "colored" nations of the world. Also, Darwin's theory of evolution was used to distinguish differences between races based on genetic branching and natural selection. This was modified in such versions of social Darwinism into the belief that the white race was the greatest because it had an attitude of superiority and a will to conquer. Such beliefs reinforced structured white power and privilege. White dominance was considered an example of natural law—survival of the fittest. Race became a societal manifestation of identity and differences, with the white race on top and other races perpetually at the bottom. Also, race became the biological placeholder that labeled and categorized one's intelligence and human potential within society. As Thompson (2005) explains, "The racial classification developed during and after the colonial era ordered races into a system which claimed to identify behavior expectations and human potential, and hence carried with it an implication for a hierarchy of humankind" (61). The design of racial boundaries was a deliberate attempt to separate inferior and superior races to encourage and legally engrain the principle of purity within a race paradigm. Advocates of a multiracial category strengthen the ideology of biological race when they use notions of hereditary determinism, such as blood quantum and superior versus inferior mixed-race unions, in their alleged "advocacy" for mixed-race people.

There is a debate among the advocates and the refuters about the degree to which even the discussion of multiraciality reinforces existing races as pure, fixed, and static categories (Chandler 1997). The history of the construction of the black and white races, for example, reveals that these groups are anything but pure, fixed, and static. In fact, their construct has been complicated, messy, arbitrary, and political. For example, in order to be classified as white in the United States, an individual needs to have white ancestry. However, through the "one-drop rule," or hypodescent, even one black ancestor classifies an individual as black. Hypodescent reinforces a race essentialist ideology intended to maintain white racial purity because it focuses on the inheritance of only the lowest-status race of one's ancestors. Also, Thompson (2005) explains the concerns over mixed-race people as the pollution of the purity of both races. As Zack (1995) points out, "Race always means pure race, the opposite of race is not racelessness but racial impurity" (301). Further, as Goldberg (2001) states, "The concern over race increasingly became about the nature and discipline, aesthetics and morality of public space, about who can be seen where and in what capacity. Thus, the moral panic over miscegenation was driven not simply by the distributed imaginary of mixed sex, with the feared moral degeneracy of black bodies consorting with white, though it was clearly that. Increasingly, such panic was expressed as anxiety regarding mixed offspring, and so the makeup and look, the peopling of and demographic power over public space" (179). Furthering this point, Thompson (2005) says, "With society divided in broad strokes of black and white, any instance of racial mixing was deemed to be a threat to the purity of the white race" (71). More important, the idea of race purity was originated to deny mixed-race people access to privilege in colonial times, such as freedom from slavery (Spickard 1989; Williamson 1995). The boundaries among races were solidified through rules of hypodescent and miscegenation as entrenched mechanisms to protect white purity and privilege. Race essentialism reinforced and reproduced the discourse that multiracials are problems because they are marginalized between two or more races. Stonequist's (1937) "Marginal Man" was a devastating image for mixed-race people. It cast mixed-race people in the role of being "hopelessly maladjusted," which supported the race essentialist discourse that unions between "inferior" and "superior" races create offspring who do not know their place and the world and are thus lost souls.

Just as troubling, the advocates, as a group, do not link their efforts with any broader racial or social justice efforts, such as the movement to abolish racial categorization altogether. Furthermore, the advocates are obscure on the political articulation of multiracialism as well as the effort to use the resurrection of racial classification to lessen racial tensions instead of in the service of self-interest.

A refuter's stance on a multiracial category is that mixed-race people should choose an existing racial category. The category they select should be dependent upon a mixed-race person's racial inheritance. This inheritance includes social affiliation, behavior, place of residence, and occupation. For example, censuses from the 1920s through the 1960s assigned monoracial status to off-spring of "mixed-blood" unions. Racial assignments were based on various factors in addition to perceptions of phenotype. Morning (2003) explains that a mixed-race ancestry could be assigned based on a status position of high or low: "Individuals of White and Indian origin could be designated as white if their communities recognized them as such, and those of indian [American Indian] and black origin could be recorded as indian [American Indian]. In contrast, mulattos were afforded no such options; no amount of community recognition could legitimate the transformation from black to white" (47). However, in the 1930s many of African descent were reclassified as Negro as opposed to American Indian. In all, it is estimated that 75 to 90 percent of the black population is mixed race although historical practices of race construction have lumped them together into a monolithic black category (Wright 1994).

Race historically became naturalized with political positionality. Furthermore, the discourse of race essentialism and racism only reproduces and reinforces the concept of borderism or racial categorization. This tendency ignores how the process of labeling oversimplifies the ways race is experienced and the complexity between individual and social definitions of race. A review of racial essentialism literature finds a lack of dialogue regarding the fact that essentialist thinking and language are so deeply embedded in our society that many new political movements, such as advocacy of a multiracial category, will continue to recycle ideologies upholding a racial categorization that protects white privilege and power.

Jones (1995) critiques the essentialist articulations of many mixed-race advocates: "Are we [i.e., multiracials] special? The census movement and its 'interracial/biracial nationalists,' as I refer to them playfully, claim biraciality as a mark of 'racial' singularity, one that in America (where most racial groups are multiethnic and multicultural) has little grounding. Their insistence of biraciality's unique status borders on elitism. They marvel at the perks of biraciality: That biracials have several cultures at their disposal. Can you fight essentialism with essentialism? Are we to believe that all biracials are chosen people, free of prejudice, self-interest, and Republican Christian fundamentalism?" (58–59) Jones's point of view directly challenges the political divisions created by a polity of multiracial nationalists who contradict their own stated beliefs by substituting one race essentialist notion for another. Therefore, the distinctions based on multiracial labels become political tools to measure strength of identity and how society parcels out resources and privileges. While embracing white notions of race cataloging, some races, such as blacks, are trapped by a system that serves to reinforce what racists have long advocated. In this regard, white definitions of whiteness and race are the determinant of racial status based on race essentialism. A multiracial category, as it has been positioned, is a danger to authentic antiracist endeavors.

In pushing multiracials to pick an existing racial category, the refuters of a multiracial category appear to be arguing for a type of "strategic essentialism." Spivak (1995) argues that strategic essentialism is "risking essentialism" as a useful tool to achieve social aims and/or goals; essentialism is at times necessary for political action. Strategic essentialism calls for individuals to be accountable to members of a social identity group to which they belong in order to create an organized social movement. The argument is that though an individual can be a member of a number of social identity groups, some identity issues need more immediate attention than others. Therefore, an individual would, to a certain extent, subordinate some identity issues to others for the purpose of political pragmatism. A strategic essentialist view of multiracialism asks mixed-race people to make a political choice and choose sides, so to speak, for the greater cause of antiracist action. After all, multiracial people already exist within the recognized racial groups.

A multiracial category brings to the forefront the power inherent in names, labels, and especially the meanings attached to them. As Thompson says, "Racial identification also presents a practical problem. Racial identification is problematic in terms of labeling because it involves labeling oneself and the people with whom one identifies. This creates the same problem as in any situation. People interact through the filter of the label. They make assumptions about each other" (2005, 104; see also Stubblefield 2001, 341–68). Thorton (1992) brings out an important point: "By definition, racial labels are tools used to categorize and to separate and/or exclude" (325). A refuter's strategic race essentialist view, though well intentioned, functions to separate distinct racial groups because its focus is on the "proper" placement within a racial group rather than the interracial politics between groups that are part and parcel of the divide and conquer strategy of white supremacy. As such, refuters advance the political and social agendas of the dominant group because they fail to explore how "choosing sides" may accomplish little in undoing the differential statuses of the races.

Multiracial discourse also supports a color-blind agenda. Color-blind ideologies assert a race-neutral social context that stigmatizes attempts to raise questions about addressing racial inequality in daily life (Bonilla-Silva 2001; Taylor 1998). Color-blind ideologies tend to substitute cultural racism for older notions of genetic or biological racism, creating a filtered vision of America in which individuals are allegedly evaluated by the content of their character rather than the color of their skin (Bonilla-Silva 2001). In reality, supporters of a color-blind ideology are primarily whites who discount the existence of systemic racism and structural white privilege. Color-blind ideology normalizes whiteness, thereby reinforcing and reproducing a system of racial division. Individual acts of discrimination are not isolated aberrations but rather reflect a larger white hegemony (Taylor 1998). Taylor further explains, "The danger of color blindness is that it allows us to ignore the racial construction of whiteness and reinforces its privileged and oppressive position. Thus, whiteness remains the normative standard and blackness remains different, other, and marginal. Even worse, by insisting on a rhetoric that disallows reference to race, blacks can no longer name their reality or point out racism" (123).

Color-blindness results in the evolution of new forms of racism, including the whitening of immigrants and reclassification of many newcomers as white or something close to white. Bonilla-Silva and Embrick (2006) describe "a three-tiered 'new racial reality' as (1) creating an intermediate racial group to buffer racial conflict; (2) allowing some newcomers into the white racial strata; (3) incorporating most immigrants into the collective black strata" (37).[1] As a result of racialized labeling within society, the acceptance of a buffer group status has led to new specific racial codes that now allow some to become newcomers into the White racial strata while others are deemed as the collective black.

This means that the one-drop rule has, at least for now, been modified. One possible reason for this is that in the 1960s whites felt pressured to give in to the civil rights demands of people of color and were not able to bring in a large group of white immigrants, as they had in the past, to form a large white coalition to subdue people of color. Miller (1992) describes how ancestry is centered on the preservation of the social power of the dominant (white) society: "Part of the function of the 'one-drop rule' . . . was to preserve the purity of white society, and thereby limit access to economic (and political) control by people other than whites. When a relationship exists of economic dependency by one group on another group, an interracial or interethnic background may be stigmatized because it represents a threat to the controlling group's power" (26). The one-drop rule is thus a manifestation of white political power within a given historical context. That historical context has now changed. Whites now need those who may not have been seen as white under the one-drop rule to become members of the white race, or at least close allies, in order to create a dominant antiblack racial coalition.

The refuters of a multiracial category advance a different color-blind point of view. Dalmage (2003) explains that many color-blind advocates suggest that their policies protect individual liberties in a society that asserts that ace does not matter nor determine social outcomes. Zack (1995) included the following testimony of Carlos Fernandez on behalf of the Association of Multiethnic Americans (AMEA) before the Subcommittee on Census, Statistics and Postal Personnel of the US House of Representatives. Fernandez (1995) argued for the acceptance of a multiracial category that would assist those of multiracial classification to "avoid unnecessary and unwarranted government influence and interference in the very sensitive and private matter of personal identity" (195). Fernandez's statement highlights individual liberties rather than social justice for group liberties. Another example of individual liberties would be Root's (1996) "A Bill of Rights for Racially Mixed People": "I have the right . . . 'instead of' we have the right," which, according to Omi and Winant (1994), is a micro-level perspective of the social process of racial formation that is individualistic and that also supports individual liberties rather than social justice for group liberties.

A more appropriate contextualization of the notion of liberty is Roberts's (1997) suggestion: "Liberty protects all citizens' choices from the most direct and egregious abuses of government power, but it does nothing to dismantle social arrangements that make it impossible for some people to make a choice in the first place. Liberty guards against government intrusion; it does not guarantee social justice" (294). In other words, individual freedom more often than not has negative consequences for others. Having the freedom to choose a racial category does little to change material racist practices of discrimination, inequitable housing, and employment opportunities. Dalmage's (2003) and Roberts's (1997) arguments are similar in that they agree that government support for color-blind policies only reproduces and reinforces a system of white supremacy because the material and ideological conditions are not changed.

Another contradictory yet characteristic debate surrounding a multiracial category involves the use of multiracial identity to expand the boundaries of whiteness. Gallagher (2004) argues that the white racial category is expanding to include ethnic and racial groups recognized as socially, culturally, and physically similar to the dominant group. Throughout the history of the social formation of race, groups that were once on the margins of whiteness, such as the Greeks, Irish, and Italians, are now part of the dominant group. The advocates of a multiracial category are rearticulating racial meanings for a multiracial identity, which will create opportunities for some light-skinned, middle-class Latinos/as and mixed-race Asians for inclusion as their ideological views of other mixed-race people and monoracials are transformed in the new tripartite racial system. Also, Gallagher (2004) suggests that as a result of the expanding boundaries of whiteness, "those groups that do not conform to cultural and physical expectations of white middle class norms, namely blacks and dark-skinned Latinos/as who are poor, will be stigmatized and cut off from the resources whites have been able to monopolize" (60).

Advocates of a multiracial category have not attracted a diverse participation racially or socioeconomically to their movement. Instead, a multiracial category serves the social and political agendas of specific camps to create a new form of racial classification that is masked to embrace a racial hierarchy and a biological construct of race. As stated previously, some groups, such as lighter-skinned Hispanics and Asians, have become "honorary whites" and would likely classify themselves as white if they had white ancestry (Allen 2005; Bonilla-Silva and Embrick 2006). However, darker-skinned individuals would not be allowed that same privilege. The larger argument is that while there are rising rates of intermarriage that may indicate fading group boundaries for certain racial groups like lighter-skinned Hispanics and Asians, the experiences of blacks and multiracials with black heritage will often be the opposite: they will find increasing boundaries, such as the changing political attitudes of nonwhites. Although there may be an increase in intermarriages and thus mixed-race babies, a multiracial category can still function as a political symbol for the emergence of a white/nonwhite divide in which blacks will remain disadvantaged relative to other groups.

Alliances between whites and nonblacks help to reinforce the normalcy of whiteness. They also further create a divide between honorary whites, blacks, and dark-skinned Latinas/os because these new honorary whites are given privileges and access that is unavailable to other nonwhites. For example, DaCosta's (2007) findings on the trajectory of intermarriage suggest that "Asians and Latinos in the United States have fairly high rates of outmarriage (compared to African Americans) . . . Almost 30 percent of Asians (27.2 percent) and Latinos (28.4 percent) outmarry while only 10.2 percent of blacks do. Intermarriage rates with whites for Asians, Latinos, and American Indians are comparable to those of Southern and Eastern European immigrants in the early twentieth century who, through intermarriage with American-born whites, expanded the definition of who is white. Latino and Asian intermarriage appears to be following a similar trajectory" (9). According to the 2000 census figures, blacks are less likely than Latinos and Asians to identify as multiracial. DaCosta states, "Of all those who reported being black, 4.8 percent indicated multiple racial identifications compared to 13.9 percent of Asians" (9). Also, the Latino identification of "some other race" category was 17.1 percent (9).

Gallagher (2004) suggests that once whites and nonblacks establish similar ideological beliefs, interracial relationships between members of these groups and blacks will come to an end. The outcome of disenfranchising blacks is to create political power alliances in numbers to maintain white privilege and reproduce the racial hierarchy. For example, Gallagher states that a 2000 study by the National Health Interview Surveys allowed mixed-race participants to select more than one race. But it also asked them to indicate their "main" race, that is, the race with which they most identified. More than 46 percent of those who marked white and Asian as their racial identity chose white as their main race, 81 percent of those who identified as white and American Indian marked white as their main race, and only 25 percent of those who marked black and white chose white as their main race. In the 2000 census data, 48 percent of the Latino population identified as white. Furthermore, Root (2001) suggests that the remnants of caste status remain most attached to people of observed or perceived African or black descent because race is still a factor in our nation's racialized history, as suggested by the Nation Health Interview Survey data. The essentializing of multiracials, that is, acting as if all multiracials experience race the same way, thus conceals that multiracialism hides the growing divisions between black and nonblack realities.

Bonilla-Silva and Embrick (2006) predict that the expanding boundaries of whiteness will in the next few decades include "traditional whites, new White immigrants, assimilated Latinos, some light skinned multiracials and some Asian Americans" (33). These boundaries are drawn based on emerging changes in the perception of phenotypic characteristics. For refuters of a multiracial category, the expansion of the boundaries of whiteness and multiracial identity choice will become a process of "whitening" to uphold white ideological dominance with an exacerbated antiblack sentiment. It is foreseeable that lighter-skinned mixed-race people will aspire to become increasingly white generation after generation by choosing partners who are lighter-skinned or white. For example, Williams (1992) found that white/ Asian biracials tend to see their racial mix as more glamorous than the blend of black/Asian biracials. Looking to the historical construct of race in the United States in which groups are distinct and well-defined entities, this would mean that exhibiting phenotypic characteristics similar to the dominant model of being human and adopting the ideologies of that model create opportunities to acquire class elevation, greater economic and political participation, and the whitening of peoples who were previously nonwhite.

Refuters have a valid point when they argue that the advocate's call for a fluid, interchangeable individual identity choice is a form of seeking whiteness. I agree with Texeira's (2003) fears of the advocate's political agenda: "My deepest fear is that the multiracial agenda will come to dominate racial discourse and research in the not too distant future. I believe this fear is well founded because of the growing numbers of racially mixed and European American researchers whose mostly middle-class backgrounds give them greater voice and whose work may be more acceptable because this discourse is less likely to challenge institutional racism and its most harmful effects" (33).

The advocates' resurrection of racial classification as an antiracist agenda can enable the development of a discourse that promotes collaboration among all races to promote racial equality. If indeed the multiracial debate is about the individual versus the group, the problem of individual identity choice for multiracials, and thus members of all racial groups, is the actual act of classification itself. I disagree with DaCosta's (2007) suggestion that the problem of individual identity choice for multiracials lies within the "new experiences" of classification that have evolved from changes within the existing political, demographic, and social context. I argue that racial classification is not new and has been interwoven within the foundations of our society. DaCosta's "new experiences" are more accurately termed "quasi–old experiences" with a new façade.

But the advocates grossly overstate the potential effect of creating a multiracial category on the overall classification scheme. To the advocates, multiracial people are difficult to classify. There are no specific boundaries. Root (1996) reiterates this sentiment when she asserts that multiracial people blur the boundaries between races. However, the fact is that these blurred boundaries only continue to assert the very existence of racialized boundaries. After all, the boundaries between races have always been blurry at the borders, yet this blurriness did not sabotage the classification scheme itself. Root's justification of a multiracial category merely reinforces a racialized hierarchy of "us" and "them" as blacks, descendants of blacks, and those deemed "honorary blacks" are inevitably positioned at the bottom of the racial classification scheme (hereditary determinism, lighter skinned versus darker skinned, etc.).

Furthermore, Root (1996) asserts that mixed-race people "have the right to change . . . identity over a lifetime—and more than once" (13). As a result of colonization and slavery, blacks and descendants of blacks have not been given the privilege to "change identity" even though "mixed-blood" unions of blacks with whites and nonwhites have shaped the ancestry of most mixed-race people in the United States. Regardless of the history of multiraciality, blacks are deemed both monoracial and impure.

Racial classification schemes of the "us" and "them" variety are often not negotiated, especially for mixed-race people with black ancestry. Lawrence (1995) refers to this status as two-faced hypocrisy: "Why is it two-faced hypocrisy? On the one hand, the dominant culture says you are less than ideal because you have a drop of 'black' in you, or a 'touch of the tar brush' in your ancestry, and no amount of 'white' blood is good or strong enough to outweigh that stain. On the other hand, that same dominant culture also says that the more 'white' blood you have in you, the closer to the 'white' ideal you are, the more we will let you into positions and maybe our houses, but you and your progeny can never attain the ideal status of 'white-ness'" (28). With race and individual identity choice of multiracials linked to white hegemony, those who maintained a monopoly over truth have defined the meaning of being mixed race. For example, white hegemony plants in the minds of whites and many nonwhites the idea that whites are superior and people of color are inferior. Power can thus be seen as more than simply a force exercised over individuals in society; it permeates social interactions and produces discourse. It creates structures to regulate and script actions and identity choices of individuals and groups. The disenfranchisement or alignment of certain racial groups through a multiracial category is one example of a consequence produced by white hegemony.

The popularity of a multiracial category and individual identity choice has resulted in a growing body of research. Much of this research focuses on reporting mixed-race peoples' claims about the impact of imposed monoracial labeling within high schools, colleges, and universities as well as its influence on their everyday personal experiences (Bettez 2007; Calleroz 2003; Corrin 2009; Lopez 2001; Lyda 2008; McQueen 2002; Moore 2006; Munoz-Miller 2009; Potter 2009; Renn 1998; Sanchez 2004; Storrs 1996; Thompson 2005). Given the rarity of research focusing on the agency of mixed-race students within a hierarchical white supremacist social structure, the overwhelming picture that this body of research paints of mixed-race students is that they are one-dimensional victims of racial labeling. In contrast, few empirical investigations of mixed-race students have explored how they use their mixedness to gain racial advantage over those with lower social status. For example, to what extent do mixed-race peoples' knowledge of and interest in the social and political realities of a racial hierarchy explain their racial identity choices?

The empirical research within high schools focuses on the effects of monoracial labeling on students' self-definition. However, some empirical studies of multiracial college and university students concentrate on their awareness of the opportunities available to them through the manipulation of identity choice as a tool for personal advantage. They also look at how the racial milieu of institutions of higher education pressures mixed-race students to choose monoracial alliances. The research conducted in higher education institutions thus differs significantly and importantly from that which has been conducted in high schools.

McQueen's (2002) study focuses on exploring the lives of racially and/or culturally mixed individuals. It looks at the relationship between cultural identity and the education participants received in the greater Toronto area. Her study was conducted through a mixed-methods approach (i.e., both quantitative and qualitative methodologies were used). The participants were of mixed heritage, with a Japanese parent and a non-Japanese parent. The total number of participants was thirty-eight, twenty-three women and fifteen men. Their ages ranged from fifteen to forty-five. McQueen expresses her concern about the social and political influence of mixedness: "I wonder how society will perceive my son. More importantly, I wonder how my son will come to identify himself. As a mother and also a teacher who interacts with students with diverse backgrounds, I have been wondering what the lives of racially/culturally mixed individuals are like" (1–2). This statement also shed lights on her motivation for doing the study.

McQueen's work shows that the complexity of identity issues cannot be examined without reflecting on the multilayered dynamics of lived, everyday experiences in a particular place and at a particular time. Since students' everyday experiences occur in political institutions that are influenced by societal norms, McQueen used an expanded definition of education that included any learning gained from any experiences students had in school settings. Although McQueen's interviews indicated that a significant portion of her participants demonstrated a sense of "not-belonging," close to half of all participants experienced some form of preferential treatment. As Cummins (1996) argues, "Schools reflect the values and attitudes of the broader society that support them and students' ethnic identity can be endangered during this process of devaluation at schools" (3).

It is also worth noting that McQueen argues that reeducating to erase bias can change the schooling experiences of mixed-race students. She believes that acknowledging and affirming the existence of mixed-race students and addressing their cultural needs can create a more positive learning environment.

McQueen's study, however, failed to ask participants their views about other racial groups. This is important to note since racial identity is a relational phenomenon. My research will fill this void, but will also ask specific questions about racial identity choices and group associations in both formal and informal learning environments. Since both formal and informal environments involve social relationships and peer influences, it is important to examine how schools as social institutions reinforce and reproduce white spaces (Allen 2006). I also asked specific questions about whether students viewed racial identity as being fluid or fixed, and allowed participants to define the meaning of those terms.

According to most comprehensive studies to date (Bettez 2007; Calleroz 2003; Corrin 2009; Lewis 2005; Lopez 2001; Lyda 2008; McQueen 2002; Moore 2006; Munoz-Miller 2009; Potter 2009; Renn 1998; Sanchez 2004; Storrs 1996), based on a comparative analysis of research that focuses on mixed-race students, no clear-cut statements make comparisons of the influences of individual identity choices within institutions. For example, Lopez's (2001) mixed-method analysis studies how high school freshman at one racially/ethnically diverse high school in California experience racial and ethnic identification, when filling out forms as well as in everyday life. Lopez's data included survey results from 638 freshmen and interview responses from a subset of 24 mixed-race and multiethnic adolescents. Students tended to see race as more "primitive," "made-up," and "less real" than ethnicity. And mixed students indicated that notions of racial categorization and phenotypic appearance motivated other students to ask the "What are you?" question. Mixed-race students sought to remedy this situation through taking particular types of action. As Lopez explains, "They talked about factors influencing shifts or changes in how they identify themselves, such as moving to more racially/ethnically diverse schools (often at junior high level) or areas/neighborhoods, learning more about their family racial, ethnic, and/or cultural backgrounds, or learning about outsider perceptions of their race/ethnicity." Lopez also found that mixed-race students based their identity choices on a variety of factors: "They talked about using a range of strategies when answering race and ethnicity questions on forms, from thinking about the context to purpose, to considering how others see them or would identify them, to responding based on what they feel 'more of,' to randomly selecting one of the categories that apply to them or responding based on their mood/feeling" (335).

Further, through everyday life interactions of identification, Lopez explored how mixed-race high school students talked about the benefits and advantages of being mixed. As she explained,

> Many of them expressed pride in being different (especially in contrast to being all or just White) and for having more or interesting culture (particularly in contrast to being just American); they also believe that belonging to

multiple race/ethnic groups gives them an enhanced ability to appreciate other viewpoints. And, while some of them said that being mixed helps them fit into multiple social groups, others found it difficult figuring out where they fit in, particularly with regards to peers, friends, and various strands of their families. For example, they described how appearing white or light-skinned can be an advantage. (2001, 215)

Also, some of the mixed-race participants indicated an understanding that "outside perceptions" shape their racial self-identity.

Lopez's findings are important and relevant to the field of multiracial identity choice in that they show how mixed-race students look upon their racial identity choices as having beneficial advantages. For example, Lopez found that mixed-race participants (1) indicated an understanding of "outside perceptions" of race and how these perceptions can influence their racial identity choices, (2) recognized that some people have more racial identity choices than others, and (3) used their mixedness as a catalyst for a fluid and interchangeable identity. These findings suggest that mixed-race students are aware of the social and political implications of how they self identify and the privileges to be gained depending on which identity they choose.

Lopez gave both a macro and micro perspective to her findings. For instance, her student participants shared no consensus in their definitions of race. Also, the participants' understanding of how race and ethnicity are socially constructed varied. Lopez explained that "blood/biology, phenotype, culture, ancestry, geography and social relations" are the determinants indicated by student participants for racial/ethnic mixedness (2001, 178). Overall, the participants interpreted and reacted to race/ethnicity definition questions in varying ways, differing not only from one another but also at the individual level—self-identification varied across situation or context. Lopez also explains that mixed-race high school students "often conform their identifications to meet the assumptions of others and other students resist, identifying in opposition to these outside perceptions" (215). This explains how society, schools, and communities influence the racial identity choices of mixed-race students. There is an underlying mechanism that is serving to reinforce and reproduce mixed-race identity choice based on a system of white supremacy.

Lyda's (2008) correlational study explored the relationship between multiracial identity variance, college adjustment, social connectedness, facilitative support on campus, and depression in multiracial college students. A total of

231 students between the ages of eighteen to twenty-three from numerous universities across the United States completed online surveys. Of the 231 students, 199 participants represented 57 different unique racial combinations, indicating a racially diverse sample of multiracial college students. The multiracial identity component of Lyda's survey was developed for the purpose of assessing each participant's self-reported identification. The social connectedness of each participant was measured on a scale (1 = strongly agree to 6 = strongly disagree) based on the degree of interpersonal closeness experienced between participant and his or her social world (i.e., friends, peers, society). The college support of participants was measured by a questionnaire created specially for the purpose of this study to measure participants' utilization of campus support services and groups/organizations. College adjustment was measured using scores from the student adaptation to college questionnaire (Baker and Siryk 1984).

An important finding of Lyda's (2008) study was the noted difference between a participant's self-identity and his or her perception of society's view of that self-identity. There was a clear discrepancy between how participants identified themselves racially and how they perceived others categorized them racially: "Participants believed that 'society' most often categorized them in a monoracial category, with 47.2% of the sample endorsing *Traditional Non-white*, and 17.6% endorsing *white*. As such, there appears to be a gap between multiracial persons' awareness of their own identity options, and what they believe others recognize as their identity options" (69). Across all contexts of Lyda's study, the results emphasized the role of phenotype as a significant factor that influences self-identity and how others perceive one. It is also worth noting that her research unveils the contextual concept that "phenotype can be both a social facilitator and/or barrier to racial group acceptance and affiliation. And as a result, phenotype can influence a multiracial student's self-identity, as well as the identity of others (particularly monoracial others) projected onto them, causing racial socialization dilateic that can shape multiracial students' identity" (70).

Further, Lyda's (2008) findings also indicated that multiracial identity across various contexts was not related to adjustment, social connectedness, depression, or the influences of facilitative supports, indicating mixed-race identity is fluid. But her results demonstrate rather than refute that phenotypic appearance and race discourse play a significant role in how one is perceived by self and others based on one's mixedness. The missing variable of this study is an analysis of the deeper meaning of mixed-race identity politics of certain race mixedness and how such a dichotomy mirrors situational identity choices in political institutions that are often not fluid for everyone.

Munoz-Miller's (2009) study focused on a baseline survey, collected in 1999, and two follow-up surveys collected from 2000 and 2004. Each survey contained measures designed to assess sociodemographic characteristics as well as psychosocial and academic functioning. In sum, Munoz-Miller's study in year 1 comprised 219 participants, 171 participants in year 2, and the longitudinal data set had 174 participants. Through the use of statistical analysis, the study explored the incidence and proportion of identity types and assessed the predictive relationships between the included net vulnerability and American Indian was viewed as of paramount importance.

Munoz-Miller's (2009) findings indicate that nonblacks identified with more than one group, whereas black/non–American Indian and black/American Indian groups were more likely to identify monoracially. Because of the pervasive presence of social structures, skin color often returned race discourse to the topic of physical appearance. One must acknowledge that in the case of mixed-race people, skin color alone often assigns a racial identity. Although skin color is a part of race, many argue that they are not synonymous. In equating the role of political institutions to so many variables of societal structures, there is a real significance to race structures in society and how mixedness as well as skin tone are crucial factors in racial designation. The various gradations of brown skin and the numerous descriptors applied to them are very important factors in the external classification and self-classification of mixed-race people.

There were also other measures that influenced self-identification choice: age, gender, status as a first- or second-generation multiracial individual, self-perceived facial skin tone, academic achievement, and perception of the oppression of nonblack minorities in the United States. Findings, in turn, revealed that first-generation nonblacks were nearly thirteen times more likely than second-generation nonblacks to identify monoracially (Munoz-Miller 2009). Specifically, second-generation nonblacks were significantly more likely to identify as multiracial. In other words, the belief that non-blacks are as oppressed as blacks in American society "led non-blacks to maintain multiracial identities rather than monoracial or inconsistent identities in

Year 1. No significant relationship between oppression perception score and identification choice was found in Year 2" (151).

Findings within black/non–American Indian groups for generation status, program status, skin tone, and oppression found that those of the second generation or later were eight times more like to identify monoracially. Those with self-reported darker skin tones were significantly more likely to identify as monoracial. Munoz-Miller (2009) found: "Adding oppression perception increased the strength of the relationship between skin tone and self-identification choice. Specifically, darker students were more likely to maintain singular than border identities. In other words, believing that non-blacks are as oppressed as blacks in contemporary American society was associated with maintaining a border identity rather than a singular identity among black/non-American Indians. This result is similar to that found in the non-black group" (153). By and large, among blacks/American Indians, racial self-identification choice was impacted by perception of oppression and skin tone.

Munoz-Miller's (2009) study provides profound inroads into the analysis of mixed-race identity influences based on mixedness. Her contributions have created a new lens outside of past empirical research that race is fluid and interchangeable for mixed-race people. Although to a certain extent mixedness creates an avenue for inconsistent identity choice based on the political and social context, it also creates opportunities for a race discourse that analyzes why in some cases mixedness has less material value. This is particularly true since the number of multiracial students emerging in America's public political institutions is growing so rapidly that researchers have predicted by 2050 they will be recognized as a significant majority (Winters and DeBose 2003). To date, the fact that little knowledge of how a multiracial identity choice can significantly impair the capacity of educational institutions to establish an appropriate race discourse in order to identify the academic strengths and needs of multiracial students is indicative of our society's inability and unwillingness to address race-based discrimination.

Potter's (2009) exploratory case study approach compared the different practices of two states in the collection of data on multiracial students in schools to determine how public policy decisions regarding accountability affect the reporting of educational outcomes for multiracial students. A comparative analysis was conducted in California, which does not have a multiracial category for data collection for student achievement, and in North

Carolina, which does have such a category for purposes of determining academic proficiency levels in accordance with the No Child Left Behind Act and adequate yearly progress targets.

The study encompassed two semistructured group interviews conducted with public policy officials in the state departments of education in California and North Carolina. The data collected focused on scaffolded semistructured interviews, student assessment data, the gathering and analysis of documentation, and archival records. Potter's (2009) comparative qualitative research is a valuable analysis of how race plays a significant role in public policy decisions. Potter's findings are centered on how public policy decisions regarding academic accountability are affected by the reporting of educational outcomes for multiracial students. She found that to date, federal educational public policies have yet to comprehensively implement a common practice of accounting for multiracial students by allowing for standardized mixed-race classification. More important, a major finding of this study is that "federal public policies have the most significant bearing on whether or not multiracial students and their educational needs are rendered visible or not" (198). A particular multiracial identity choice can determine which mixed-race groups' (i.e., black/nonwhite versus white/Asian) needs are "rendered visible or not."

Potter's (2009) study of the emerging mixed-race student population in political institutions will contribute significantly to research on the specific needs of multiracial students to guide the educational community in the development of curriculum, social and emotional necessities, and staff professional development involving this group of students. The research findings indicate that multiracial students are visible when it comes to accounting for their achievement in schools. The question at hand becomes how will public policy redefine current constructs of race, racial identification, and racial classification?

Corrin's (2009) study contributes in two ways to data on multiracial youth: it explores schooling experiences and analyzes data from a sample drawn from populations of seventh to eleventh graders in multiple cities, providing for an extensive comparison of many types of monoracial and multiracial youth. Corrin's sample comprised 40,373 respondent surveys measuring academic success. The three highest-scoring groups were Asian, Asian/white, and white students. The bottom four groups were black, black/Hispanic, black/white, and Hispanic students. This pattern was most pronounced for grade point average. Also, Corrin found that Asian, Asian/white, Hispanic/ white, and white groups clustered together for the school outcomes. While the black, black/Hispanic, and black/white groups tended to cluster together, the Hispanic group did so only for the outcome of closeness to teachers. For all other school connection variables, monoracial Hispanic students clustered more closely with the white and Asian groups.

In comparing multiracial group outcomes, Corrin (2009) found that Asian/ white students outperformed other biracial groups. The Hispanic/white students did significantly better than black/white and black/Hispanic students. Black/white students tended to be significantly different academically from both the black and white students. An interesting finding is that "the black-white students, who typically rank in the middle academically, score low in regards to school connectedness" (56). Overall, the significance of Corrin's study for my own is his investigation of how access to resources improves our understanding of racial group differences. More important, he looks at what connections might exist for multiracials versus monoracials to socioeconomic resources, particularly those resources with educational relevance that would impact access to school-related success. Although Corrin's study will contribute to filling in the gaps of comparative academic achievement, parental support, and connectedness to school of monoracial and multiracial students, there are also missed opportunities to analyze the socioeconomic factors of mixedness as it relates to race having material value.

Moore's (2006) research looks at the experiences of nine middle-class black/ white biracial students in an advanced educational program at an urban high school, Douglas High School. Three of the participants were male and six were female. All were over the age of eighteen. Moore's study used qualitative methods to gather information through formal interviews in which participants reflected on their high school experiences. She found that biracial adolescents felt pressured by peers to choose racial identities that fit the way others perceived them phenotypically. Her study also examined the way that the formal school setting—teachers, the curriculum, forms, and school activities—created a monoracial label for biracial students. Moore writes: "How race is translated in schools affects biracial students on a daily basis. The curriculum at Douglas is predominantly framed in white, Euro-American traditions, and though there are some classroom text materials focused on different racial groups, there is no mention of biracial contributions" (121). The absence of biracial people in the curriculum creates a push for monoracial labeling and a classroom environment that is not supportive in helping multiracial children develop positive self-images. Moore argues that the outcome is the denial of mixed-race people in the United States that serves to protect a social order that relies on clear racial boundaries. Further, Moore asserts that "the student participants described how being monoracially labeled by others and categorized into a monoracial identity affected how students felt in school and how they defined themselves" (122). Her findings also indicate that biracial individuals are forced to live within "color boundaries" created by the social construction of race. As a result, the biracial participants created a self-image that was affected by how others categorized them racially.

Also, the assumption that mixed-race people tend to view themselves as victims is a result of most either denying or not being aware of the possibility that they are actually assisting discrimination and privilege relative to other racialized peoples. Moore (2006) suggests that multiracials see that they have "crossover power" in "playing the race card." As Moore says, "The first advantage [to being multiracial] is probably the most obvious to others and that is they get to 'play the race card'" (2). Later, Moore writes, "Crossover power or not being definable by others" is an example of asserted advantage of a mixed-race identity that supports color-blindness. In both situations, the students use multiracial identity choice as a social and political benefit, yet the students act within the confines of a racial hierarchical classification scheme to choose an identity that fits the particular situation and environment by reinventing a status quo, a continued stigma of race. For example, Jordon, a participant in Moore's research, uses his light skin tone to navigate between racial groups and boundaries. He says, "You can pretty much do whatever you want when you're biracial. I'm pretty sure I can go join the Asian Association and say that I'm Sri Lankan and no one would question me. It's nice to have brown skin and not to be so definable. It's an advantage when I first walk into a room and not know anybody and I don't have a group I'm supposed to fit into" (74).

Another example in Moore's research of using multiracial identity choice as a social and political tool is a mixed-race student choosing a black identity to get into college. As Moore reports, "He said he does not feel it is fair that his White friends do not have this same advantage, even though they may have higher qualifications to get accepted" (2006, 73). From this perspective, Moore asserts that mixed-race students use their mixedness as an advantage and are not affected by how others will be left to stand alone against racial inequality through their racial identity choices.

Moore's findings indicate that eventually her participants came to understand their own identity through a multiracial lens, embracing the hope of a "raceless" society that supports the idea that everyone will be equal. The key findings of Moore's study are: "(1) biracial individuals live between color boundaries; (2) biracial people are 'colorbound' by a monoracial system; (3) biracial people are labeled monoracially by institutions; (4) some individuals believe they are 'colorblind' and so being biracial is not an issue; (5) biracial people learn to define themselves as multiracial; (6) society and schools continue to use monoracial labeling and categorizing; and (7) multiracial individuals have a dream for a 'raceless' society (2006, 124–131). Moore's research offers strong, relevant content on the experiences of mixed-race students, but it also has limitations. First, Moore does not explore the possibility that mixed-race students' advantages are the result of their own racial opportunism. While she acknowledges that multiracial students do operate in this manner, she does not see it as problematic. Second, she does not critique the participants' dream for a raceless society, given that they demonstrate racial opportunism themselves. The participants do not problematize the fact that their own beliefs and actions perpetuate the higher social status that they hold over other racial groups.

Lewis (2005) conducted a qualitative study of three schools. One, Metro2, was an alternative, progressive school with a Spanish-immersion program and large Latino student population and staff. Although it was a school in a Latino neighborhood, it had a significant number of white students whose parents wanted them to learn Spanish in the immersion program. Lewis's research at Metro2 was set primarily in a classroom where English was the language of instruction, but the significance of her study was the role of whiteness in this classroom and in other spaces at the school. The "outside perceptions" at Metro2 created "white spaces" even though the school was only 30 percent white. Lewis states, "Even in a place like Metro2, where people imagined themselves to be antiracist, whiteness still functioned as a symbolic resource, providing all those who possessed it with the benefit of assumed knowledge and ability" (126). For example, Lewis describes the racialization process of a multiracial student at Metro2: "Hector was the son of an El Salvadoran father and white (European American) mother. In a conversation, Hector's mother reported her son's frustration that teachers considered him White and assumed that his first language was English. Though Hector was read as white, he was proud of his Latino heritage and of his skill with Spanish. Though his teacher might not deny his Latino ethnicity, in casual classroom exchanges he was regarded as distinct from dark-skinned, working-class Latino children. Thus, no matter how he envisioned himself, Hector was generally associated with whiteness" (125). This is an example of how a student's self-concept of his identity clashes with pressure to conform to an identity ascribed to him. Examples such as this reveal the persistent power of racialization in the daily influences of schools. In this case, teachers continued to use whiteness as a symbolic point of reference in their perception of Hector's racial place. He was differentiated as being apart from and superior to dark-skinned Latino children. Lewis's research reveals the role that schooling plays in the active racialization of student bodies, sorting them into racial polities with varying levels of power and status.

A different example in comparison to Lewis's study on identity politics influenced by societal measures of race would be Phinney and Alipuria's (1996) mixed-method study. Their participant sample consisted of 194 ethnically or racially mixed high school students with a comparison sample of 696 monoracial students from the same school. Their results indicate that 34 percent of the students used spontaneous self-labels of mixed heritage, whereas 66 percent of the respondents used a monoracial label associated with one parent. Most nonblack multiracial students with a white parent often identified as white, which created distorted dispositions toward other groups, such as less positive views of monoracial black students. Also, it was perceived that mixed-race students' decisions to attend a predominantly white university versus a predominantly nonwhite university were determined by their self-label, and that label itself was influenced by various factors. The pattern of which mixed-race students were more likely to attend white universities opposed to non-white university was based on factors that influenced their choice of self-label. For example, physical appearance is a factor that shapes self-label. Those who have identifiable black features are usually labeled black, regardless of whether other types of features symbolizing a different group membership are also evident. Further, the use of a white versus a minority self-label by mixed-race respondents on predominantly white campuses was related to their choice of community, which means that they conform to the race composition of the campus. As mentioned previously, not all mixed-race people will have the choice of self-label and the result would be choosing a university on the basis of their predominant race identification.

The limitation of Phinney and Alipuria's study is the lack of connection they make between the agency of self-labeling and the macro racialized social system. In what ways did participants' self-labeling represent conforming to or resisting a white supremacist structure? In ignoring the social and political structures of race within this study, the results normalize the notion of pressure to identify in terms of monoracial hyperdescent because the political realities of the larger, hierarchical social order are discounted.

The research on mixed-race students in higher education offers different perspectives on the influences of learning environments on individual racial identity choices. Renn's (1998) qualitative study used ethnographic methods and grounded theory analysis to research the experiences and racial identification preferences of multiracial college students on a predominantly white campus. Renn's twenty-four participants were from three undergraduate institutions: Carberry, an Ivy League college; Ignacio, a Catholic university; and Wooley, a liberal arts college. Renn found that a key factor in how students racially identified was based on "where they felt like they fit in, which was determined largely by the messages they get through the mesosystem of peer culture. It was a matter of trying to figure out not only where they could fit in, but also where they felt like they belonged to a group" (150). College students were sometimes aware of the racialized opportunities available to them through their choice of college. Several students selected their colleges because they believed that they could find certain kinds of welcoming community spaces. For example, Renn explained, "Dan wanted to explore his Chinese heritage and selected Carberry in part because it had an active community of Asian students. Kayla was looking for people who would be a 'good influence' on her. Phil chose to live on the multiracial floor at Ignacio because he wanted to be part of a diverse residential floor dedicated to exploration of pluralism" (144). For most students, the desire to find a place to belong was critical in their decision to attend a particular institution.

Sanchez (2004) conducted a qualitative study of multiracial identity expression in a university. She used interviews and self-report questionnaires with a participant sample that consisted of thirty-one multiracial students at the University of New Mexico. Her study explores the factors within a university setting that promote or inhibit the development of a multiracial identity. Some of Sanchez's participants felt that the tension between racial groups at the university inhibited the expression of a multiracial, as opposed to a monoracial, identity. For example, "groups formed cliques, segmenting the student body primarily by racial and social groups" (161). As one of Sanchez's participants explains, "From what you hear, there is a power struggle between Native American, Hispanics, and Anglo groups within the state and I think that is reflected here in [the university] as well. And I am not part of that . . . Unless you fit into one of those three groups, and African Americans too . . . well, not unless you fit into one of those three groups, you are pretty much separated. You are isolated within you own little sphere" (161–162). A different reflection by another participant reinforces the existence of racial tensions: "If you go out there between classes, you will see that most [of] the black guys who are athletes—I don't know if all guys I see out there are athletes, of course—but they congregate in one part, away from the rest. And you see a lot of the white guys and girls, many of them who are in fraternities or sororities, that all congregate on this other side . . . but if you look you can see that they separate from each other" (163). In this example, the climate of the university influenced the individual identity choices of multiracials to choose racial alliances. By giving space for the creation of separateness between groups and encouraging intraracial alliances, cliques on campus were mostly based on monoracial grouping as races competed with one another. Also, Sanchez found that "participants did not generally discuss identity politics in relationship to their personal choice for affiliation; however, they recognized that they played the system to their advantage." As Sanchez says, "Multiracials problematize classification systems because visual reading (Racial Readings) no longer accurately represents a specific racial group. For example, Darrell, a white-black male, was usually read as white due to his skin tone. Nonetheless, participants used their racial composition to maximize societal benefits" (209). The defined boundaries of racial groups, highlighted in a college or university environment, provide a context for mixed-race students to actively participate in racial identity politics.

One unique finding in Calleroz's (2003) qualitative study is how the racial identity choices of ten multiracial college students were shaped by the racial organization of their peers. Calleroz notes that their "acceptance into or rejection from a community often determined the crowd with which mixed-race students connected and hung out." Calleroz's study describes the experiences of students with their peers: "It is clear that initial interactions were based almost exclusively on visible appearances, and more precisely, visible differences" (123). Dominic Pulera (2002) illuminates the negative aspect of visible differences that reproduce and reinforce inequalities within racial groups: "Observable differences in physical appearance separating the races are the single most important factor shaping intergroup relations, in conjunction with the social, cultural, economic, and political ramifications that accompany this visual divide. These dynamics animate the unceasing struggles for power, recognition, and resources that occur between, among, and within American racial groups" (8–9).

Participants in Calleroz's (2003) study often experienced how visible differences automatically provided group membership and simultaneous exclusion from other groups. For example, a mixed-raced black and Hispanic participant describes her nonwhite group membership as a result of visible differences based on the expectation to reflect what society views as black, in terms of both appearance and behavior. Once the participant included her black ancestry in her mixedness, she found herself dealing with the racial dynamics between the campus's racial groups. It is clear that the visible differences of mixed-race students were instrumental in students' alliances with or disenfranchisement from various racial groups.

Perhaps one of the most important messages of this line of multiracial research is that mixed-race people use their mixedness to become fluid or interchangeable; they learn how to navigate within the confines of a racial hierarchy. Racial identity choice is used as form of agency to access skills, resources, and social capital. One way that multiracials, especially multiracials with white ancestry, maneuver the racial terrain to their advantage is by relying on their relative white/light skin privilege. Most will use their relative whiteness as a tool to provide them access to enter white spaces. Bettez (2007) conducted a qualitative study of sixteen multiracial participants living in Albuquerque, Boston, or the San Francisco Bay Area. The racial mixedness of her participants included black, Mexican, Peruvian, Filipino, Somali, Japanese, and white ancestries. One of Bettez's participants, Tina, exemplified how a multiracial person uses her whiteness to "pass," thus gaining relative advantage: "Tina 'passes' everywhere she goes; she is perceived as white. Although she doesn't primarily identify as white, and in fact in several instances in her interviews talked about how she considers herself primarily Mexican, she recognized that other people identify her that way. She takes her liminal space as a white-looking, Mexican-identified person and uses her white privilege to be an ally for people of color" (179). Although Tina portrays herself as an "ally" she also distinguishes herself as different from people of color by not openly revealing her status as a mixed-race as opposed to white person. Because she uses her "visible differences," a person of a darker skin complexion is not on an equal level with her. Her skin complexion places her in a position of power in relation to those who cannot access white privilege.

Storrs (1996) explored how thirty women with mixed racial ancestry identified and the reasons for their individual identity choice. Participants were recruited through snowball sampling methods from three cities in the Northwest: Spokane, Washington; Eugene, Oregon; and Seattle, Washington. Storr's study chose these sites because the Northwest locations share a common regional racial history and makeup. The participants belonged to one of two groups: a younger cohort of mixed-race university students and older mixed women.

Whiteness for many of the mixed-race women in Storr's study was associated with racism, patriarchy, and oppression. The oppressive nature of whiteness was conveyed through their personal stories. One of her participants had a Chinese mother and a black father. Storr describes how the hypodescent legacy of the one-drop rule erased the participant's Asian ancestry because her racial identity "was based on her mother's understanding that race and racial designation was determined by the father's race" (1996, 119). This story exemplifies how some race groups are more disenfranchised than others due to the political, social, and economic ramifications of being racialized. Also, this reiterates the oppressive and discriminative aspect of blackness and how the individual identity choices of multiracials can reproduce and reinforce the material benefits associated with their nonblackness.

Although most of the authors I have reviewed in this chapter agree that mixed-race people use their mixedness in ways that are fluid and interchangeable, the authors did not connect this to the larger picture of how racial identity choices support racial power structures within both informal and formal learning environments. The phenomenon happens across regions and grade levels. Therefore, it is important for schools to be attentive to mixed-race identity choices and create more awareness and education about mixed-race issues. The school is one of society's most powerful institutions in reproducing and reinforcing systems of white supremacy. If schools became more aware of mixed-race identity choices, it could impact the biased beliefs and prejudices of other racial groups. Since it is in school that mixed-race students most often choose racial identity choices, teachers and administrators need to be prepared to assist them throughout their schooling experiences. It is important that educational programs begin to address the issues of race in society to become aware of how schools, peers, administrators, and teachers influence and racially label students. The all-important first step is educating people about the social formation of race and its power structures, elucidating how racialized discourse is used to create expectations of how others appear, act, and behave.

The school is the primary institution where young people are categorized and sorted according their racial status (Lewis 2005). Schools can be empowering if they inculcate pride in one's history and respect for others'. But this is rarely the case. Although antibiased and antiracist education is a step in the right direction, schools need to take a more active role in supporting racial identity choices of multiracial students that take account of the racial hierarchy. It is important to question how mixed-race students' enactments of individual identity choice influence their schooling experience by either conforming to or resisting racialized social structures within learning environments. As discussed in this review, there are underlying mechanisms that influence the racial identity choices of multiracial high school students. And while a more open system of choice can be positive, these choices must be made in ways that do not reinforce the devaluing of racial groups with lower social status. Moving forward, my research will fill a necessary void connecting the racial identity choices of mixed-race students to the perpetuation of the racial organization of the United States.

## Note

1. The collective black strata is a nonwhite group in a tri-racial stratification system with whites at the top. The tri-racial system in the United States includes "blacks, dark-skinned Latinos, Vietnamese, Cambodians, Laotians, Hmongs, Filipinos, New West Indian and African immigrants, and reservation-bound Native Americans [American Indians]" (Bonilla-Silva and Embrick 2006, 34).

# 3

# Methodology of Study

Due to the limited literature available, this qualitative study is somewhat exploratory as it seeks to understand the perspectives of mixed-race college students' racial identity choices. I relied on a qualitative case study method of conducting interviews and groups sessions for data, and then used qualitative approaches to analyze, interpret, and present the data.

This study is qualitative because of its emphasis on how reality is perceived and experienced by the individual participants. Creswell (1998) defines a qualitative case study as "an exploration of a 'bounded system' or a case (or multiple cases) through detailed, in-depth data collection involving multiple sources of information rich in content" (61). The essential component of my research is an attempt to create a space for my participants to dialogue. As the researcher, I then became "the conduit through which such voices can be heard" (Denzin and Lincoln 2000, 23). Ultimately, my research aims to contribute to emancipation from the generations of silence maintained by those who find no solace in the racial structures perpetuated in US schools.

DOI: 10.5876/9781607325444.c003

My research included opportunities for participants to represent their ideas in response formats, such as through conversations. The participants and I met for discussions and interviews in a private conference room on campus. It was important to establish a convenient but private setting to help foster a sense of community among participants and to increase the likelihood that they would feel safe engaging in conversations about being mixed-race, a subject so often foreclosed in schools. The meeting room was intended to be a place where students individually and collaboratively could make sense of the racialized social structures within schools, communities, and society.

One critical aspect of this study was that participants' words were understood to be shaped by larger political discourses. My role was really more than that of a reporter; I was also a social critic. My beliefs are necessarily situated in a particular worldview and ideology. Creswell (1998) reminds us of the political nature of qualitative research: "Qualitative researchers approach their studies with a certain paradigm or worldview, a basic set of beliefs that guides their assumptions" (74). Furthermore, as Denzin and Lincoln (2000) note, "Behind the terms [theory, method, analysis, ontology, epistemology, and methodology] stands the personal biography of the researcher, who speaks from a particular class, gender, racial, cultural and ethnic community perspective" (18). As such, my lived experiences as a mixed-race educator and qualitative researcher are entrenched in this study. As a researcher, I viewed myself as working out of a critical race paradigm, which I used to affirm or critique participants' discourse.

As an educator at Cliff View College (the name is a pseudonym), I had access to mixed-race students, so I began seeking among these for participants willing to share their experiences. I opted to use the "snowball" technique as a means of finding mixed-raced interview subjects. Meetings with potential participants took place in November 2008 on the Cliff View campus. During these meetings, I explained the project in detail, answered questions, and distributed to interested students a packet containing a participant consent letter, a demographic questionnaire, and a self-addressed, postage-paid envelope. I plainly described my goals for the project in the consent letters so the participants were informed about the objectives of the study from the beginning. Potential participants were given a week in which to complete and return the forms. (I also provided the participants with a duplicate consent letter to keep for their own records.)

After the deadline for returning forms, I processed the consent letters and participant demographic questionnaires received. I used the questionnaires to interpret how well each prospective participant fit the required profile of my study (e.g., all participants must have two or more racial heritages). The participants included individuals whose parents are of two or more socially designated racial backgrounds. The final number of students who fit the profile and agreed to participate was nine.

The participants I selected identified as American Indian or acknowledged American Indian ancestry. They came from various tribal communities. All were students at Cliff View College in New Mexico. Cliff View College was opened in the 1960s with funding from the Bureau of Indian Affairs. The college proclaims that is embodies a bold and innovative approach to education. The unique learning environment of Cliff View College seeks to promote American Indian/Indigenous leadership and an atmosphere that allows students to embrace their cultural heritage. At the time of data collection, the school enrollment was 513 students, representing eighty-three federally recognized tribes and twenty-two state-recognized tribes. In the 2008–2009 academic year, 89 percent of the college's students were American Indian. The students had the choice of residing on or off campus.

To protect the anonymity of my respondents, a pseudonym is assigned to each. Given the character of qualitative research, learning more about each participant was imperative. I offer below brief portraits of all nine participants. A chart outlining a brief summary of each student is found in appendix C.

## Tony

An older student married to his Navajo wife for twenty-four years, Tony has three children (a son and two daughters) and a grandchild. Tony identifies himself as outspoken and a loving father. He was born in Los Angeles and attended Centennial Senior High School. In earlier years of his life, he lived in Chinatown, then Gardenia. His memories of school include being bused to Compton to attend school, where his friends were "pretty much a melting pot."

Tony has always acknowledged being mixed-race, but his mother urged him to "be a strong black man . . . you are always going to be viewed as a black person because people view your skin before they view everything else." This molded his self-perception of being raced as black. As Tony says,

"Some people would automatically and readily assume that I'm black. I have no issue with that."

## Stacey

Born in Phoenix, Arizona, Stacey self-identifies as Navajo. She stated that she is proud to say she is Navajo and reared traditionally within her culture. Although she does not speak her Native language fluently, during her childhood she was surrounded by family members speaking Navajo. She has a close relationship with her Navajo mother. And she attended Monument Valley schools, which emphasized culture and tradition. She proclaimed with a passion, "I love crocheting!"

As a mixed-race person who identifies as American Indian, Stacey revealed that she often felt she was not accepted by her father's family (white/Hispanic) and was ridiculed by her peers at Native-oriented schools for being mixed (German/Mexican). "I'll introduce myself . . . like, in Navajo, you know . . . say my clans and as soon as, like, people hear, like, German or Mexican . . . they're like, 'What?' You know when they first hear German, they called me a Nazi." Her willingness to share her American Indian peers' perceptions of her identity brought up questions about blood quantum and the meaning of Indianness. Regardless of her experiences, Stacey is very proud to acknowledge that she belongs to two clans, her mother's (Navajo) and then her father's (Hispanic/white).

## Anthony

Anthony has a bubbly personality that shapes his entire outlook on his lived experiences. Anthony identifies as being a "very" fair-skinned Hispanic with a multiracial heritage of Hispanic/American Indian/white. Most of our conversations began with Anthony sharing chocolate and his recent comic art sketches.

Anthony spent most of his childhood in a multicultural setting on a navy base in Pearl Harbor, Hawaii. He did not become curious about his identity until his family relocated to New Mexico. He described the state as not having a "mixture of cultures," stating it was "more like its own culture." His father's admonition to "be proud of your last name; carry it forever" has had a profound impact on his identity. To lighten the tone of our conversations, Anthony would always add humor. When I asked him what people assumed about his race, he said, "Well, in Hawaii, when I was going to school there, I knew I was Hispanic because my Dad told me to be really proud of it. But whenever I would tell people, they would say, 'Oh, you're from Mexico?' People just don't understand!"

Although Anthony has a lighter outlook on life, he has had significant experiences of being raced. Once he was judged by his last name when applying for a job; the interviewer reacted to his fair complexion with surprise when they met: "Oh, you're Anthony." Anthony concluded, "Am I gonna get graded badly because of my last name? But it's something that can happen . . . you know?"

## Samantha

Fair complected with straight hair, Samantha at first seemed shy and reserved. But very soon she was at ease, rattling off details of her school, family, and schooling experience with little prompting.

She acknowledged that she is half Navajo and half white. Like many students in this study, she discussed her experience of being raced while attending a private school that was predominantly American Indian. "They all saw me as white and treated me like I was white." Though most of her friends were American Indian and white, Samantha says that her school experience influenced her racial identity. Although she had some negative experiences being mixed race, she does not judge people based on their race.

College has been a significantly different experience for Samantha than for some of the other participants. She feels more accepted and does not think other students view her as being white only when she is with American Indian peers.

## Kathy

With a smooth brown complexion and dark eyes that convey a strong sense of self-confidence, Kathy is an older student who was reared by a family from the Southeast that acknowledged only their black heritage. She explained that her family sees identifying with American Indians as taking "away from how they see themselves or who the public sees them as."

Kathy has a wealth of experience of identifying as a mixed-race American Indian; because of her phenotypic features, she often is made to feel that she has no claim to being American Indian. Because she is not an enrolled member in a state or federally recognized tribe, her Indianness is further questioned by her peers and in her classroom and campus experiences. Kathy expressed a great deal of frustration about how she will be perceived as an artist, especially as an American Indian artist creating traditional art. She remembers being asked, "You're not *all* black, are you?" Her experiences have not hindered her passion for Native cultural activities and embracing her heritage through traditional art forms.

## Logan

Logan would stand in my doorway, tall and brown, with a confident smile. He could be described as an activist for American Indian people, a student leader, and definitely the devil's advocate for our conversations about mixed-race experience. Half white and half Creek, he identifies as American Indian. He acknowledged that in his hometown mixed-race people with American Indian heritage variously did and did not identify as American Indian.

Logan stated he never experienced having to prove his status as a mixed-race person who identifies as American Indian. "I was of the opinion that I didn't have to try to be Native . . . I just was Native." Because Logan phenotypically fits the mold of "looking" American Indian, his identity was not questioned. This was one of many reasons he could play devil's advocate, often saying, "Why can't you just be Native and not worry about how people view you?" However, he did acknowledge that there are issues with "skin color," which can often be a factor in whether or not others perceive you as being American Indian.

## Kim

Kim identifies as Alutiq, but has a mixed-race background of Alaska Native and white. As an Alaska Native, Kim has a great appreciation for the environment and its significant impact on the culture of her people. Discussing mixed-race identity, Kim noted that her sister is Alaska Native/black/white and there are no issues of race in her family. Her smiles were unquestionably full of excitement when she shared personal stories about salmon fishing with her boyfriend or snowboarding on fresh powder.

In many conversations, Kim openly admitted that she missed home and did not understand why people on campus "judge each other with their eyes." She thought her peers judged people based on their phenotypic appearance without making attempts to get to know them as human beings. Lacking a sense of belonging on campus because she was from Alaska, Kim often did not attend class or preferred spending time with her boyfriend. During our last conversation, she revealed that she had decided to return home to Alaska.

## Jennifer

Jennifer has Puerto Rican roots. At school, Jennifer identifies herself as both Indigenous (Taino) and Hispanic, but in Puerto Rico it was forbidden by her family to identify with Taino heritage. In Puerto Rico, the elders know the Taino language and culture, but it is viewed problematically as being without value. As a result, her family encouraged her to identify as Hispanic.

Jennifer's choice to attend a tribal college created awareness in her of blood quantum issues within tribes in the United States. She discussed how some of her mixed-race friends are "frustrated about how people are viewing them and how they want to fit in." Most of her conversations on the American Indian identity of her mixed-race friends revolved around blood quantum questions and feelings of needing to prove their identity. On campus, Jennifer has a grounded self-perception: "I just be myself. I don't have to carry a feather in my pocket." Her priority as a student is academics.

## Amy

Amy identifies as mixed-race, but in our conversations she switched back and forth in saying she was Hispanic or American Indian. She is very fair complected with light brown hair, giving her an advantage in situating herself. Throughout our conversations she talked about her Kiowa influences and the meaning of family. Her schooling experiences included describing her friends as Mexican, even though she admitted that they preferred to be identified as Spanish.

I collected data from these participants in several ways: semi-structured, audio-taped, individual interviews, one conducted at the beginning of the study and one at the end; audiotaped whole-group discussions; reflective researcher notes; and the researcher's personal journal. After consent was secured from each participant, I scheduled meeting dates and times to interview each participant individually. All participants were reminded that they had the right to refuse to answer any questions. I encouraged participants to be forthright and honest. I explained to them that they should not let my personal association with them influence their willingness to share their personal experiences. In order to develop a rapport with each individual prior to whole-group meetings, the first set of individual interviews focused on the students' racial ideas and experiences. I asked participants to reflect on and respond to questions on identity that emphasized parents/family/home, peers/friendships/dating, and school (e.g., "What racial identity choice do your parents encourage?" "Do you have friends who are mixed?" "In school, what do people assume about your racial identity?").

I next conducted whole-group discussions, recording these dialogues. The group sessions asked participants to reflect on and describe identity and lived experiences (e.g., "Are there mixed-race people who used their mixedness as an advantage?" "Are there hindering actions by others toward mixed-race people based on their phenotypic features?"). It was my goal that group dialogue would serve as a safe opportunity for participants to raise issues about their heritage, their identity choices, and the racial measurements they experienced in school. My status as a mixed-race educator and my dedication to taking data interpretations back to the participants for validity ensured that the space felt safe. The private setting of the discussions added to the feeling of safety. The collected data were used as texts for analysis.

In the individual interviews at the end of the study, participants were asked questions about how schooling affected their racial identity choice and race consciousness (e.g., "Do you think you act differently around people depending on their race?" "Tell me about a time in school when you changed your racial identity choice to feel accepted or comfortable among peers or teachers."). In these interviews, as in the first ones, I used open-ended and clarifying prompts, asking questions that encouraged participants to discuss their important lived experiences as mixed-raced students. The individual interviews were semi-structured to allow for a more conversational, shared experience.

The interviews [appendixes A and B] lasted between twenty and thirty minutes, and group sessions from sixty to ninety minutes. I took minimal notes during the individual interviews and group sessions to avoid disrupting the comfort of open dialogue. In each interview, participants were asked the same questions, with opportunities for expanded conversations as needed. All interviews and group sessions were transcribed and analyzed, with special emphasis on conversations pertaining to how mixed-race students see themselves and what they experienced as mixed-race students conforming to or resisting racial privilege in an informal and formal setting.

In this research project I used the standard research practices as described by Creswell (1998). Data collected from multiple resources were coded, organized, and condensed into descriptive categories and subcategories (Creswell 1998). Then, I made a comparison and linked the categories and subcategories to pinpoint patterns of descriptions as well as inconsistencies.

My qualitative data analysis was based on data shrinking and interpretation, with the goal of identifying categories and themes. To analyze the data, first I went through each transcript (of interviews and group sessions) and highlighted answers to those questions. Second, responses to those questions that were found to be of interest for the questions being investigated were highlighted. Third, a summarizing interpretation of each highlighted statement was made, thus creating three overarching themes: how mixed-race students and peers perceived themselves; how mixed-race students were raced; and the classroom and campus experiences of mixed-race students. Fourth, the list of themes was copied into separate charts, laying out each participant's answer to each question of interest. Fifth, from the list of themes, each participant's combined statements of lived and schooling experiences were studied and categorized as conforming to or resisting race privilege, with supporting quotations as evidence.

# PART II

# AMERICAN INDIAN MIXED-RACE EXPERIENCE

# 4

# Racial(ized) Self-Perceptions

It evident that what happened in participants' lives before they arrived on a college campus was crucial to their college experience. The students articulated the influences on their sense of mixed-race identity, particularly family influence and the impact of their schooling and peers. While most students attending college have certain expectations and experiences, mixed-race students attending an American Indian institution have a unique multiracial experience shaped in interaction with the normative monoracial notions of American Indian culture and traditions that exist at Cliff View College. These types of normative notions of culture and tradition are mediated through the racial lens of "hereditary determinism," which is an ideology rooted in the belief in and aspiration to "pure" blood quantum and an allegedly superior same-race parentage versus inferior mixed-raced parentage (Cramer 2005; Garroutte 2003). Those who can claim pure blood status are seen as being more culturally "authentic" and hence "traditional," thus linking notions of race with ethnicity.

Since race is a product of white privilege and power, the discourse of mixed-race students at Cliff View College can also be described as acknowledging

DOI: 10.5876/9781607325444.c004

races as categories that our society invents and manipulates to reinforce a white supremacist belief in the inherent inferiority of people of color. Logan explained, "I am Native American. I am white. I am both. I am neither. When I hear people criticize white people . . . I am reminded of what I am. In fact, more and more tribes are starting to go white; it's the popular trend." This trend can be seen at the micro level as an individual act of race being used for self-interest or for social and political gain (Omi and Winant 1994). Logan's statement that "I am neither" supports the race politics that are controlled by macro forces that operate beyond the micro individual racial identity. However, it is important to note that Logan's comment that "it's the popular trend" for tribes to align themselves with whiteness only pinpoints how some tribes attach importance to the reality of whiteness within a racial hierarchy and, in turn, contribute to the construction of white supremacy through aspiring to get closer to its ways and appearances. As we shall see, Logan's comment also provides a guide for understanding why certain mixed-raced students at Cliff View College use particular discourses to navigate the racial politics of the institution.

The mixed-race students in this study acknowledge that many at Cliff View employ the idea of hereditary determinism, which places people into fixed, seemingly natural racialized categories. Many students who identify as being full bloods or who phenotypically fit the stereotype of being American Indian (brown complexion, straight, dark brown or black hair, braided hair, etc.) have already negotiated their racial identity prior to arrival at a tribal college. Through their negotiations, mixed-race students have actively participated in race essentialist notions that one's membership can be questioned if one does not possess the essential physical traits. Race essentialism, a primary tool of hereditary determinism, is used as a mechanism of social division and racial stratification. For example, Logan stated, "I used to think that light-skinned Natives were posers. I still mostly do. However, it isn't their fault they were born pasty." As Thompson (2005) explains, "The racial classification developed during and after the colonial era ordered races into a system which claimed to identify behavior expectations and human potential, and hence carried with it an implication for a hierarchy of humankind" (61). The choice to actively negotiate a racial identity as a "mixed-race" person is a deliberate attempt to separate inferior and superior unions within a race paradigm in that it reifies the notion of purity, or "non–mixed race." In fact, the degree to which a mixed-race person negotiates race only reinforces existing races as pure, fixed, and static categories (Chandler 1997).

For example, Logan described hereditary determinism through a race essentialist lens of the "already negotiated racial identity" and expectation of being a student at a tribal college: "Full bloods and those who are phenotypically completely Native . . . sometimes do carry a chip on their shoulder. You know . . . like, you owe me . . . I'm full blood . . . I've got it owed to me and that's why I'm gonna excel . . . you should give it to me."

Similarly, many mixed-race students who identify as Native American or acknowledge their Nativeness have been functioning within their comfort zone relative to their choice to identify as mixed race. The choice of attending a tribal college places mixed-race students in a position of negotiating their identity yet again. Nonetheless, at Cliff View only certain forms of racial mixedness are allowed the opportunity to negotiate identity, that is, to claim both Nativeness and mixed race. Mixed-race students who phenotypically appear black have added challenges relative to those who appear non-black that make it difficult to claim Nativeness or, for that matter, mixed-race identity. The overall seemingly immutable imbalances of power predetermine the mixed-race experience at this tribal college, often revolving around the conceptualization of the social and political politics of Indianness. The larger picture of power imbalances at play indicates how the in/authenticity of Indianness is defined by whiteness and how white supremacy "determines relations to power, the re/production of labor divisions and property, the construction of social status, and the context and script of race struggles" (Allen 2006, 10).

Logan's references to "posers" and "those who are phenotypically completely Native" are examples of how the power influences of whiteness have changed the meaning of Indianness over time, but also affected the power relations and the social status of imagery of the authentic and inauthentic identity of Indianness. As Deloria (1998) explains, "The authentic, as numerous scholars have pointed out, is a culturally constructed category created in opposition to a perceived state of inauthenticity. The authentic serves as a way to imagine and idealize the real, the traditional, and the organic in opposition to the less satisfying qualities of everyday life. The ways people construct authenticity depend upon both the traumas that defined the maligned inauthentic and upon the received heritage in the authentic past" (101).

The problem posed in this study is that the long-standing race politics of authentic versus inauthentic Indianness has become redefined around a new set of concerns, that is, the identities of mixed-race American Indians (Cramer 2005; Garroutte 2003). The influences of the power dynamics of whiteness have become ingrained in the meaning of Indianness. Students' mixed-race identity choice at Cliff View can then be viewed as a struggle with the "interior and exterior Indian Others" (Deloria 1998) or, in other words, as conforming to or resisting a racialized social and political structure that places a material and symbolic value on the Indian-as-nature. Whites project onto those they have constructed as "Indian" what they believe they have lost via modernization; to the white imagination the "Indian" must embody oneness with nature so as to counterbalance the banality of modern white existence. Thus, whiteness associates purity, in both cultural and racial forms, as closeness to nature, a nature that is eroding due to the excesses of development.

Studies of mixed-race identity choice do not necessarily focus on how a certain identity choice can be viewed as either conforming to or resisting a racialized social and political structure. And most studies do not seek to show how schooling experiences influence mixed-race students' racial identity strategies. This study sought to fill that void. Through interviews and group sessions that focused on students' mixed-race experiences, it became apparent that their racial self-perceptions were developed in response to social interactions in which various social actors assigned or ascribed certain mixed-race identities. In other words, they were "raced."

The issues at hand for self-perception are not only mixed-race identity strategies but how race is viewed as being "real," not a concept based on white privilege and power. Students in this study described their experiences from early childhood to the present. They identified as one race, one race and mixed race, both races, or mixed race. Factors that impacted the identity choice of mixed-race students' identity included physical appearance, others' expectations, and affirmation or rejection by peers.

## Identity Politics of Blood Quantum

Mixed-race identity can be seen through a colonial lens that began no later than 1705 with blood quantum laws or Indian blood laws: legislation enacted to define membership in American Indian groups. "Blood quantum" refers to attempts to calculate the degree of tribal racial inheritance of a given individual. Virginia adopted laws in 1705 that made both a person of "American race" (which at that time meant "Indian") and a person of half-American race (i.e., a "half blood") legally inferior. However, the notion of blood quantum was not widely used as overt public racial policy until the Indian Reorganization Act of 1934 whereby the US government documented whom it considered American Indian.

Furthermore, when the US censuses were taken in 1930 and 1940, many mixed-race people of black and American Indian descent were classified as black. Racial classification based on the one-drop rule has negatively affected many individuals with black and American Indian descent because they are unable to prove residence on a reservation or prove that they meet the required ancestry to be enrolled in a tribe.

The societal and political experiences of American Indians and blacks today are very different. "Indianness" is often exoticized, whereas "blackness" is denigrated. Society teaches us to categorize people so we understand who they are, what stereotypes they fit into, and how they should act and we should act toward them so that they can be kept under control. One of the primary societal categories used as a form of control is race. Among my participants, the most glaring difference in racial(ized) self-perceptions existed between those who identified as black/American Indian and nonblack/American Indian. As their experiences reveal, blackness affected racial identity in ways not perceived by the simple mathematical proportions conveyed through blood quantum, meaning that the one-drop rule seemed present in how blood quantum and cultural authenticity was *socially practiced.*

Tony has always acknowledged being mixed race, but his mother's warning that "you are always going to be viewed as a black person because people view your skin before they view everything else" molded his perceptions of being raced. He shared an anecdote from his family history illustrating the point:

> I remember hearing a lot of stories . . . My grandmother . . . my mother's mother, is very dark. You know, but when you look at her, she does not look typical of a Native southern black woman. But then again her daughter is very light, and I remember even when I was a kid we used to walk down the street— they used to say . . . you know . . . nice friend . . . this . . . this and that . . . My mother was born when my grandmother was fifteen years old. So their ages

are really close. And she would say . . . "No, that's my mother" . . . What! And you could see the shift . . . everything is cool and then she says, "This is my mother" and then it freaking happens . . . there is a line drawn.

Tony's story is an example of the perceived biological aspects of phenotype and skin tone. The reality of blackness cannot be easily separated from the issues of power that have been historically embedded in society. Tony's phrase "there is a line drawn" distinctively describes a moment of racial exclusion, the repulsion of blackness at the level of micro-aggression, which on a larger scale creates discriminatory effects for blacks and those who identify with their blackness. Consequently, the "drawn line" is the societal manifestation of the racial hierarchy at the level of everyday life, with the white race on top and blacks perpetually at the bottom.

Relationships between and among family members shaped how the students approached the issue of mixed-race identity. As Pulera (2002) notes, "Parents differ on how they acculturate their children to mixed-race identities" (40). Kathy recounts her childhood familiarity with racial politics and identity:

I remember growing up as a kid knowing that I was part Cherokee and being ashamed of it. Because . . . I mean, we are talking little kids . . . like eight . . . nine . . . ten. For starters . . . you know . . . the stereotypes I've grown up with about [how] Natives were Indians on the Plains . . . warrior . . . the fighters. The other side . . . I look at the Cherokees and they were just like the white people . . . what the hell. But there were things going on with me as a kid . . . my family was ashamed of being part Native. That sort of thing . . . you know . . . but it wasn't until later that I actually read our history.

Kathy's perspective was shaped by her family's desire for an "authentic blackness" untainted by a history of white violence. She associated Indianness with the group she was most familiar with, the Cherokees, and thus associated that form of Indianness with whiteness. This conflicted with her parents' desires for a pro-black orientation. At the same time, she had internalized negative stereotypes about American Indians in the western United States, against whom she measures the authenticity of Cherokees. Kathy also expressed dismay at the fact that people who look phenotypically white, like many Cherokees, ironically have an easier time claiming Indianness than those who look black, such as herself.

Experience with the rules of hypodescent manifested in adult family relations. Tony, who is married to a Navajo woman, describes how hypodescent plays out in his interactions with his in-laws:

Uhm . . . [my wife] has a huge family . . . half of her family is really cool . . . in general they are all cool . . . upfront and in your face. There are no issues . . . at the same time . . . it's about knowing who's who and the true mask comes off in your face and it comes out. Her older sister has really crazy issues in terms of race and I'll say . . . I would definitely have to say that she is a racist. The kids come around . . . her children and they have brothers and sisters . . . Navajo traditions and they have no problems, but I know as soon as we walk out that door . . . it's like the talk of the town. The word spreads fast and we are just like . . . wow. A lot has to do with the social class within . . . maybe jealousy . . . a lot of social class issues because you guys were in California and maybe because my wife left the reservation and . . . you know, it's like all of those issues. Besides all of that . . . the bottom line is that these guys are still part of your blood . . . this is your sister's kids . . . it doesn't matter. When my kids go over there . . . it's like . . . you can hear a pin drop and they know it, but they are strong enough . . . we have taught them well enough to where they can handle that. Well . . . that whole thing . . . it just sorta plays itself out.

Authentic Indianness is not simply about purity. It is also about what type of (so-called) impurity is recognized and what is excluded. In mixed-race American Indian identity, blackness is treated as something to be denigrated and pushed away, unlike whiteness or even Latino-ness. Being black/American Indian mixed race threatens the definition of Indianness in that it moves its association closer to that of blacks and away from nonblacks—namely, whites.

In this way, race politics, both within and between races, can determine one's experiences of racial in/authenticity. Logan, born of a full-blood Creek father and white mother, states, "I come from a divorced family. I lived with my mother, who's Anglo and part Eastern Shawnee. And . . . I was the oldest child living in the house and also the only Native American child at the time. And so . . . it wasn't much of an issue . . . I have loving and supportive family on both sides. I've been taught to be proud of all of me, both the white and Native side." As a result of how whiteness influences the power dynamics of the material values of race, Logan's authenticity is not questioned or viewed as having lower social status. This stands in sharp contrast to the experiences of Tony and Kathy. When white/American Indian mixed-race people like Logan are encouraged to be "proud of all of me" and black/American Indian mixed-race people like Tony and Kathy are given messages about the inferiority of their blackness, racial hierarchy is reinforced, a hierarchy in which whiteness increases your social value while blackness decreases it.

Samantha has parental support similar to Logan's, but different in the sense that her parents, a Navajo father and white mother, encourage her to have a fluid, interchangeable identity.

> Uhm . . . they just tell me to be whoever I wanna be. Like . . . they don't really say a specific racial type cause they know me as Samantha, not as like Navajo or white . . . so . . . they really don't look at it like that. Our extended families are pretty distant. And we really don't talk with them much anyways. Like . . . I have an aunt in Canada . . . an aunt in Utah . . . an uncle in Texas. And like . . . I'll keep in contact with some of my cousins . . . we'll say like "hey" and stuff, but it won't be like in depth at all. It just never comes up that way.

Samantha's fair complexion and phenotypically white features allow her to have a fluid, interchangeable identity, while Logan, brown complected, phenotypically appearing American Indian, is not allowed that type of flexibility. In truth, the encouragement of Samantha's parents to "be whoever you wanna be" ignores the racial constructs of whiteness and reinforces its privilege and oppressive position (Taylor 1998).

Such acts can also be viewed as a color-blind perspective that evolves into new forms of racism, expanding the boundaries of whiteness as it becomes associated with freedom of racial identity choice, so long as one is close enough to whiteness. Bonilla-Silva and Embrick (2006) describe this new racial-social reality as three-tiered, consisting of: (1) an intermediate racial group that buffers racial conflict, much like the middle class does in a class analysis lens; (2) a dominant white racial strata; and (3) a bottom-tier "collective black" strata that incorporates many dark-skinned immigrants (37). This means that only certain raced groups will be accepted as the "buffer group," the group closest to white without actually being white, while others will be deemed the collective black. The consequence is to ensure limited access to whiteness; the one-drop rule will be modified (e.g., allowing those who approximate close enough to whiteness to "be whoever they wanna be"), and blood quantum politics will heighten the manifestation of white political power within a given historical context.

Tribes will align with the white power structure to the extent that whiteness is embraced as an authentic part of Indianness and blackness is rejected as inauthentic. This racialization of authentic Indianness challenges the current new age notions of Indianness that claim that one need only be "culturally" Indian in order to be authentically American Indian (Deloria 1998). As we have seen, race is still a major component in determining American Indian identity. As one participant, Logan, described it, tribes are "starting to go white; it's the popular trend." And a major ideological feature of whiteness is opposition to blackness. A certain social and political ideology that is filtered through a larger white hegemony will take precedence to advance the mechanisms that allow for racial stratification. Once again, race essentialism will continue to hinder a stance against racism, as will inattention to the realities of racial privilege and hierarchy. As Spencer (1999) asserts, "The challenge for America lies in determining how to move away from the fallacy of race while remaining aggressive in the battle against racism" (167).

Although the students encountered different family and parental situations based on their mixedness, the prior experiences of race dynamics for all nine were relevant to how they viewed race as a symbol. Seeing race this way played into the reassigning of human value, whether it was "drawing a line" or "being ashamed" of certain mixedness. The experiences of the students might lead one to conclude that the alliances between whites and nonblacks will continue to reinforce a racial hierarchy of "us" and "them," as blacks, descendants of blacks, and those deemed "honorary blacks" continue to hold a denigrated position. Regardless of the history of multiraciality, blackness is not fluid nor does it come with an option "to be whoever you wanna be." The same was true for participants in this study who were seen as black. For all participants, prior experience of skin politics and the historical construction of race indicated how there were varying experiences reinforced by one's mixedness.

## Self-Perceptions of Race Asserted, Negotiated, and Redefined

Understanding the patterns of how race is asserted, negotiated, and often redefined for some participants provides an image of how self-perceptions of blood quantum are often used to self-label and assert, or avow, an identity. But in some cases, as in Logan's, being mixed race did not have an impact on views of "whiteness" or "Indianness."

The relationship between Logan's American Indian/white (but identifies as white) mother and his American Indian father provided him with early positive exposure to the interaction between races. While his father's family had a much stronger cultural and traditional connection, Logan did not struggle with a negative perception toward blacks or whites, being reared in a community where, he stated, "The black ghetto meets the Indian ghetto." Logan further explains,

> My white side of the family loves the fact that I am Native and . . . partly because they have the same . . . uhm . . . cultural background but it was never reported. So, because of all that nonsense that they're not Native. And then on my dad's side . . . we have just as many half Indians/half whites as we do half black/whites. So, it's just completely accepted and they love us . . . you know, just the same . . . there's no differentiation between . . . cultural worth. Just 'cause you're half doesn't make you less than a whole. Our Freedmen are still members of our tribe and I take a certain amount of pride in that because I think that's the way it should be . . . you know . . . if it was good enough for our ancestors . . . it should be good enough for us. Those people who had been descendants of slaves and were members of the tribe and then married out of it . . . chose to ignore their Creek heritage, but there are black people at home that I know are Indian. That is just how they chose to identify.

When I asked Logan how our conversation about mixed-race identity made him feel, he stated:

> It doesn't really bother me. One thing that . . . here's an interesting point . . . mixed race and phenotypically non-Native-looking people are more sensitive about their identity. And I would agree because . . . I mean that it is justified but like, someone like me would no doubt have a complete different experience than someone that looks phenotypically black and identifies as Native. I look full-blood Native . . . I come from a community where mixed race is not an issue, so I have a very unique situation where I'm accepted as I am.

So, Logan acknowledges that it means something different to be seen as black and identify as Native. Yet, Logan then went on to claim that he looked "full-blood Native" and that where he comes from "mixed race is not an issue." He dismisses his privilege, or at least distances himself from its construction, at the same time that he acknowledges it. Also, Logan disliked hearing negative comments about whites because his mother identifies as white, but he acknowledges her Nativeness. He came to accept through our discussions that the comments are a reflection of historical oppression by the larger white society.

The white preference of Logan's mother, who seemed to have rejected an option to associate with her Nativeness, simply emphasizes that whiteness is seldom questioned. And there is a history among American Indian people of encouraging the claiming of whiteness when possible. However, claims to whiteness were received selectively. Morning (2003) provides an imperative historical account that explains why Logan's mother's can identify as white while acknowledging her Nativeness: "Individuals of white and Indian origin could be designated as white if their communities recognized them as such, and those of Indian and black origin could be recorded as Indian. In contrast, mulattos were afforded no such options; no amount of community recognition could legitimate the transformation from black to white" (47). Darker-skinned individuals are not allowed the same privilege as individuals with lighter skin in American Indian groups, and thus the social structure of American Indian groups plays a role in the construction of whiteness.

Stacey's strong cultural family ties directly influenced her identity as a mixed-race person who identifies as American Indian. Probably as a result of the Navajo Nation not formally accepting blood quantum law until the 1950s, mixed-race Navajo participants had varying influences on how they perceived themselves. Stacey explains,

> I choose to be Navajo because that's how I've been brought up and raised. You know . . . my grandparents would always talk to me in Navajo when I was younger, just being brought up traditionally. So, I just consider myself more Navajo than the other races . . . German and Mexican.[1] My whole family, pretty much . . . 'cause it's like they say that if you're . . . in our clan system . . . your first clan is your mom and your second clan is your dad. Whichever is your first clan is like who you are . . . so it's like . . . my dad is German and Mexican—that's like my second clan. But my first clan is Navajo from my mom. Uhm . . . my mom didn't want me to be like, I don't know,

like going through this big old identity crisis . . . you know? She didn't . . . she
honestly kinda doesn't like white people so much 'cause like . . . some people
are just like really bad . . . you know? She wanted me to have respect for
myself . . . for my own identity . . . you know?

Stacey's family experience is an example of how one's mixedness determines
if one's authenticity will be questioned or not. And although Stacey is mixed
race (white/Hispanic), her authenticity was not questioned in comparison to
the family experiences of Tony's children, who are black/American Indian
mixed-race.

Sometimes colorism played a role in the treatment of the students.[2] There
is a racialized process of the politics of pigmentation being re-created out of
a larger context of white power dynamics. Hunter (2005) explains: "Whites
assigned meanings to whiteness, blackness, and brownness that valued them
each differently. As an abstract concept, whiteness is believed to represent
civility, intelligence, and beauty, and in contrast, blackness and brownness are
seen as representing primitiveness, ignorance, and ugliness. These abstract
concepts took on representations in the form of actual physical traits associated with each racial group" (49).

Colorism is not only an issue within the black community, it is also a determinant of social status within American Indian populations. Stacey described
her sibling's experience with colorism as a mixed-race brown person.

Something my sister told me . . . like . . . when she would meet some white
kids and stuff and, I don't know, they . . . they would be talking about races
and stuff. And . . . they would say like, . . . "Ooh . . . I'm part Cherokee," . . . say,
like an eighth or something. My sister would be like, "Well, I'm part German,"
and they be like, . . . "What? You? But your skin is really brown" . . . and
they be like, . . . "You can't be part German" . . . you know. Looking at
her like that . . . I don't know . . . when she told me that, I just kinda saw
both views . . . like from the white person trying to claim that they are part
Cherokee . . . now my sister was like, . . . "What?" But when she said she was
part German . . . you know, they were sort of really puzzled about that.

It is revealing, to say the least, that Stacey's claim to Indianness was given more
credence than her sister's claim to whiteness. The social construction of race
makes it more difficult to look past the color of skin to explain the differences

between "what are you" and "who you are." This weakens Root's (1996) assertion that mixed-race people would disrupt racial classification schemes (hereditary determinism, lighter-skinned versus darker-skinned, etc.).

Anthony describes the pressures of being raced:

> Based on appearance, I am light complexioned and I am believed to be Anglo instead of Hispanic. I had to prove my racial background to others because I phenotypically appear white. And a lot of times on standardized tests, I didn't know what to choose 'cause I was like . . . I am Hispanic but no one believes me. So, should I just put white? I don't know why I felt like that. I just always felt like I had to prove myself. Because everyone was just like, . . . "Well, you just don't seem like Hispanic" or whatever.

As a result of Anthony's skin color, his authenticity is questioned based on a reinforced racialized classification scheme. Skin color is used a reinforcement tool. The social and political forces of skin color conflict create a darker-skinned versus lighter-skinned hierarchy that defines in/authenticity for group association and membership.

Stacey had a similar experience of being raced. "First, I went to school with a bunch of Navajos . . . [who] like look at me and call me a white girl . . . you know? I was like . . . I'm not white . . . I'm half Navajo." Anthony's and Stacey's experiences exemplify how the expectation is internalized that race is a "real" concept and puts pressure on mixed-race students to choose a group associa-tion that aligns with the social and political norms of racial rules.

Kim made a racial identity choice based on how society has categorized her according to her skin color and facial features, regardless of the fact that her mother is Alaska Native/white. "Well, I actually identify myself as . . . Alaskan . . . as Aleutic . . . Alaskan Native because my dad is full, or so he says, full Alaskan Native. And . . . I just look Native, so it's just what I go by. If somebody asks me what else I was I would . . . I would tell them Russian or German because the . . . German is my last name."

Kim's decision to identify as Alaska Native aligns with what others assume her phenotypic image portrays. Kim's understanding of outside perceptions thus shaped her racial self-identity. Her situation fits that described by Lopez (2003), who found that while some participants resisted ascribed identities, many conformed their self-identity to meet the assumptions of others. The control mechanisms of outside perceptions that influence self-identity are created by societal norms, white privilege, and power. White people never have to question their racial identity, because it is expected and known "what they are." The integral nature of white privilege and whites' inability to self-reflect about the meaning of being a white person suggest there are no outside perceptions that influence "what they are." Yet, most white people know they are white because the world tells them so.

The story of Stacey's sister is similar to that of other students. Since skin color is the most enduring construct of a system of race and the most difficult to change, colorism then becomes a structural barrier to moving away from race. Logan explains a family experience of colorism and hypodescent. "My aunt has three mixed children, all from three separate black fathers. So, it's even in our own family . . . we love those kids to death, but you know . . . my aunt's mom still has derogatory comments about black people in the presence of her grand-babies. You know . . . I mean . . . I don't know. We all know that it's wrong and yet . . . it happens."

Unfortunately, the effects of blood quantum and skin color have manifested a perception of how Indianness is defined, while simultaneously, a racialized process reenacts the denigration of certain mixedness. As Lawrence (1987) argues: "To the extent that this cultural belief system has influenced us all, we are all racists. At the same time, most of us are unaware of our racism. We do not recognize the ways in which our cultural experiences have influenced our beliefs" (322).

Kathy's prior struggles over how her "blackness" shapes her "Indianness" has created an awakened awareness of how she is perceived on campus.

I think phenotypically is like—obviously they say, "She's a black girl."
Here . . . at this school . . . I wonder if it would have been easier for me to say I'm black [rather than Native]. I wonder if I would have had an easier existence here on this campus. I tend to wonder is there . . . a difference between an individual who is and how they are perceived as mixed white and Native or whatever? Is there a difference, because it seems like in my experience it's kinda like, . . . "Ooh . . . you can't be Native . . . you are part black" or "You are black" or whatever. And I'm like, learn something about your history and something about the East Coast and you might figure it out. But it seems like . . . especially here at school . . . it's like, . . . "Oh . . . well . . . you are pretending" or "You couldn't possibly be." And I'm really curious, why do people believe that there is a physiological impossibility for that mixture?

As a result of Kathy's experiences, being mixed race with black has placed her socially and culturally in an inauthentic category. Not only is she viewed as being black regardless of her mixedness, she is also not accepted into American Indian group membership, unlike nonblack/American Indian mixed-race participants.

Tony gave details of a similar experience at Cliff View:

> Most people on this campus that say that they are full blooded in fact aren't full blooded. So in class when they view someone else's opinion [as] more valid or . . . more important because I'm this or that or I look this way or look that way . . . those are the things that are just mind blowing. I shoot them down every chance I get when I'm in that type of mentality, but I don't like to be that way. Because by nature, I'm not that way . . . I'm more of an optimist . . . I try to, like, give people the benefit of the doubt until they prove themselves to me otherwise. I find that a lot of people here carry a lot of racial and prejudice baggage. And all I can say is that there is a major difference between having white blood in you versus any other type. And it draws a line even within your own race and you often question yourself a lot of times before you come to terms with yourself and feel good about yourself. You go through a lot of trauma.

Historically, people who had the slightest trace of black blood were forced into an identification category of black. The identity politics of blood quantum for American Indians has been significantly different than it has been for blacks. As a result, there is a different perception of colorism that validates blood quantum by skin color, which impairs the ability of American Indians who are mixed race with black to become a member of a group. The social and political reality of alienation for black mixedness is different from white mixedness on an everyday level at Cliff View College. Black mixed-race participants such as Kathy and Tony experienced alienation by being positioned as outsiders based on their phenotypic appearance. They are grouped as outsiders solely because they lack the phenotypic traits associated with an insider racial membership, thus challenging the notion that Indianness is practiced primarily as an ethnic or cultural identity (Deloria 1998). Phenotypic traits associated with race include skin color, hair texture, and facial features (Hunter 2005; Lee 2005; Lewis 2005; Lopez 2003).

Hall (2008) explains the identity politics of blood quantum for certain racial mixtures (e.g., white versus black mixedness) thus: "(a) African-mixed Native Americans may be seen as wanting to escape the social stigma associated with being 'black,' and (b) discrimination on basis of their dark skin may disqualify them [from American Indian membership] because of appearance; unlike their lighter-skinned European mixed counterparts, they are more physically similar to African American" (36). Under the circumstances of social and political influence, the oppressive assimilation of colorism has shaped, transformed, and constructed a racial hierarchy that validates the dominant race's categorical status. The acceptance of an American Indian whose race is mixed with white over one mixed with black has resulted in a postcolonial ideology of assimilation through white ways, culture, and racism. Hall (2008) gives an example:

> Chris Simon, a professional hockey player and member of the Ojibwa tribe, was fined $35,585 and suspended three games for apparently directing racial slurs toward a black player named Mike Grier . . . The behavior of a Native American player in a predominantly white sport is comparable to that of their slave owning ancestors, but there has also been criticism by Native Americans of blacks playing on sport teams that degrade them by the use of such mascots as the NFL's Washington "Redskins" and the major league baseball team the Cleveland "Indians." (36)

These are examples of creating alienation based on one race being "denigrated" versus the popularity and profitability of being American Indian.

Identifying as American Indian has an economic value, whereas identifying as black comes with no sovereignty or access to economic advantages. According to Vine Deloria Jr. (1999), "With the passage of the Indian Reorganization Act and the Oklahoma Indian Welfare Act, it became profitable to be an Indian" (231).[3] As a result, in today's era of Indianness, there are a significant number of people who choose to acknowledge their American Indian heritage simply to take advantage of services or special accommodations (educational scholarships, medical benefits, etc.). Unquestionably, one result of the 1980 census allowing people to identify their racial background themselves for the first time has been a change in the race dynamics of contemporary North American society. Analyzing an example of "playing the race card" in reverse, Deloria shows how self-selected identity can be used to navigate through racialized social and political barriers within political institutions: "Colleges and universities today give preference in admission to minorities, and it may well be that non-Indians, eager to obtain admission to law schools or colleges of medicines, are claiming Indian ancestry in order to leapfrog their fellow applicants who seek admission on the basis of merit alone. The American Indian Law Center in New Mexico reports that it continues to be astounded at the number of alleged Indians attending law schools in various parts of the country" (233). Both "playing the race card" and self-perceptions of blood quantum politics are racialized pressures for mixed-race students who identify as American Indian to behave or maintain group associations based on Indianness.

Logan explains his views on the strategy of cultural authenticity in gaining racial group membership:

> I find it interesting that some mixed-race individuals cling to stereotypical imagery as their connection to their cultures. We've seen the part-black woman go into ghetto mode when she's around her black friends, or the part-Native man who embraces and enhances their connection with the earth and the Great Spirit. It wouldn't bother me as much if these individuals would pick a theme and stick to it. Don't play your Eastern Band Cherokee fantasies by dressing in the Northeast style and not missing the nearest pow-wow . . . ever heard of a stomp dance in a turban, 'cause guess what? That's your cultural identity. Of course, it isn't unheard [of] to see full bloods doing the same thing, so . . . when in Rome. But . . . previously . . . I had considered it unnecessary, almost to the point of calling it a weakness. I now think that playing the race card is necessary in some respects. I feel that on a societal level, it is impossible to progress without first knowing where it is you come from. In today's society, minorities are criminally discriminated against. In that instance, I think playing the race card is justified and necessary.

Logan's comments of in/authenticity further describe the race politics of Indianness. Not only does skin color play a role in your group association, but also the politics of how one acts in a certain manner makes him or her an active participant in racialized hierarchy. Logan's perspective that "playing the race card is justified and necessary" does not take into account that playing that card only upholds being raced, while certain raced groups will be continuously denigrated.

Although Amy acknowledges her Nativeness, her ascribed lack of cultural Indianness affected her personal life.

> I grew up in Santa Fe. And very few white friends. I don't never want to date a white person because they got no culture. Uhm . . . just recently . . . like, a year ago, I was dating a Taos, a Taos Native and [he] was exactly what I wanted. He was very into his culture from one of the Pueblos. And he seemed to really respect and love that, and that's what I really loved about him. He spoke his language, which is so rare to find [*laughs*] . . . But I wasn't Native enough for him. I wasn't a little Taos girl . . . who was into doing the Taos tradition. So, it didn't end up working out and that was the main reason.

Amy was unwilling to play the "authenticity card" to become accepted and was affected by the drawing of boundaries.

Many of the participants acknowledged that to gain access to certain groups meant knowing how to maneuver through that group's particular social norms. Samantha's willingness to appear more authentic included changing her behavior and choice of conversation depending on the particular racial group with which she was interacting.

> I act differently around people depending on their race because each race of people has a different way of acting, and by acting as they do . . . then I don't offend anyone or make them feel uncomfortable. But I've always been aware that I'm mixed race, so when I'm at school I guess the only time I felt more of an award was when I was told that I looked white. I changed my racial identity by feeling more of that race. Like in Window Rock, I felt white but I would try to feel Native by playing basketball really well.

Samantha was able to navigate her group association based on her mixedness and phenotypic appearance. In her case, she had the advantage of being more phenotypically white, and she understood how to manipulate her mixedness to gain access to certain group associations. As we will see next, Samantha's experience is much different from that of a dark-complected black / American Indian mixed-race person. Black / American Indian participants had a more difficult time being included in white and, in certain situations, American Indian racial groups.

Kathy, a mixed-race person who phenotypically appears black and acknowledges her Nativeness, gave a different perspective of playing the game of

American Indian authenticity. "I'm viewed as black even though I identify with my Native American heritage more often. I don't have the option in many cases other than the fact that I identify as a mixed-race Native American that is not an enrolled member of a tribe. The catch is around black people I'm a sellout . . . meaning I look a certain way [black] . . . and . . . I identify with my Native American side." Kathy's lived experience of her authenticity, both black and American Indian, being questioned hints at the power dynamics at play in group association.

In a more resistant tone, Tony proclaims, "I can only just be me. If acknowledging who I am and where I come from to some people is playing the race card to some sort of advantage . . . that's crazy. Then, you know . . . they need to deal with their own issues. It's their problem, not mine. I am who I am . . . regardless." Although Kathy internalizes her ascribed identity and Tony refuses his, the common denominator of both their perspectives is that they have been racially positioned at a certain location within a larger racial order. Blacks see Nativeness as a higher-status location and thus challenge Kathy's identifying upward. As evidenced by the treatment of blacks within tribes, American Indians see blacks as a lower-status group. So it is not surprising that Tony and Kathy's Nativeness was questioned and often denied by other American Indians. Their reactions to exclusion and racial positioning bring to the surface the historical experiences of black mixed-race persons. Contrary to DaCosta's (2007) claim that multiraciality is a new experience, the multiraciality of today encompasses older experiences of US racial power dynamics and their role in forming group associations.

Family factors often played a role in how the participants viewed group association. Families were important in how participants came to understand the meaning and politics of phenotypic appearance within a system of colorism. Tony explains his family's perceptions of race and colorism: "I can say personally my family is a big melting pot. My grandmother was like, half white. There is a big issue with that in my family, whereas you have the dividing line between the lighter skin and the darker skin." When asked how he felt about this form of skin politics, Tony stated, "I would say the biggest pain is when it comes from your own family . . . direct immediate family. Now that's the biggest part, especially when you don't understand and it doesn't make sense." To Tony, this whole business of privileging light skin seemed absurd, especially when it involved loved ones.

This is a clear example of how skin color plays a significant role in how one views race as a byproduct of the social and political influences of a racialized hierarchy. To better understand colorism in this context, it is important to dissect the social controls of race through a Critical Race Theory lens and unveil how race is convoluted through the racial discourses of colorism Since the implications of "whiteness" are seen through a "racial perspective or worldview" (Leonardo 2002, 31), the meaning of Indianness seen through a lens of blood quantum and the "one-drop rule" shapes the perspectives of what a particular group deems as "normal" group membership characteristics. In other words, if one group is normalized based on a particular set of characteristics defined within, and by, a white supremacist hierarchical system, it causes an "action-reaction" effect of the other groups to view themselves in terms of racialized characteristics (e.g., dark versus light skin, where light skin is assigned a higher social value). For example, light-skinned slaves were sold at a higher price than dark-skinned slaves. "At slave auctions, [slave masters] would almost pay five times more for a house slave than a field slave showing that they were more valuable (a field slave could be bought for almost sixteen hundred dollars, while the going rate for a 'fancy' girl was almost five thousand dollars)" (Byrd and Tharps 2001, 19). Tony's experience of having a "dividing line" in his family based on skin complexion indicates why he would view race as being a kind of absurd game whose players "need to deal with their own issues," as if they suffered from a form of mental illness. The complex meaning of race, and its interrelatedness to skin color and hair texture, infiltrates political and social domains at the personal and cognitive levels.

William Katz (1986), the author of Black Indians, stated, "Black Indians, like other Afro-Americans, have been treated by writers as invisible" (5). Katz is criticized by hooks (1992) for not acknowledging how whiteness has made the black mixed-raced Native American "invisible." Katz's argument that "observers, not expecting to find Africans among Indians, did not report their presence" (5) understates the distorted racial history of whiteness. But his omission of not acknowledging the power structures that define being "invisible" does not capture the lens of how blackness has been denigrated historically. Tony, a brown-skinned descendant of black, white, and Native American heritage, discussed how he has experienced his invisibility as an American Indian: "I think that I don't peg myself as being 'Hey, look . . . I'm

African American.' But I . . . include . . . my total . . . you know? . . . I recognize and I do include my Native American roots. But most only see me as African American." The context for what Tony has experienced is shaped by a racial system that promotes whiteness as the model of humanity, and blackness as the opposite. The racist discrimination against dark-skinned American Indians by those who are light skinned as a result of white heritage is rooted in the same racial system that allows for the alienation of dark-skinned Native Americans on the basis of the "one-drop rule" associated with blackness (Russell, Wilson, and Hall 1992).

Jennifer, a product of Puerto Rico's Spanish, Indigenous, and African mestizaje who identifies as Taino (Native) and Hispanic, indicates how societal norms assign "whiteness" a higher value in a nonwhite group.

> The way I kinda see it . . . we still have that way of looking at people . . . you
> look at their appearance. Like if we see . . . like a black Native as opposed to
> a white Native and I think people still see white people as . . . like this symbol
> of power and strength because of that fact that they are majority. And . . . so if
> a white person will say that I am Cherokee . . . they still hold that . . . the fact
> that they are still majority and people won't say as much as opposed to some-
> one who . . . who is black and Native. Like . . . we always have prejudgments
> but kind of pretending or whatever. But we see the white person as more of a
> symbol of authority than we do the black person.

Jennifer's comment that "we see the white person as more of a symbol of authority than we do the black person" indicates that the history of mixedness in the black race has not elevated their status out of the basement. In fact, a substantial number of blacks have both white and American Indian ancestry.

Persons in New Mexico with white, Spanish, and American Indian ancestry can be considered "Hispanic" or "mestizo."[4] Similarly, in some South American countries those with black, white, and American Indian ancestry would also be labeled mestizo. For various reasons, the meaning of mestizo in New Mexico is grounded in "whiteness," making white mixedness an advantageous social power. However, those who appear phenotypically black have a more difficult time claiming mestizo status, unlike those who are light or medium skinned. Nieto-Phillips (2004) explains the New Mexican Spanish identity perspective of "whiteness": "In the quest for full inclusion in the nation's body politic, the challenge for Nuevomexicanos, then, was to establish their whiteness and, with the rise of the Mexican immigration in the early years of the twentieth century, to distance themselves from 'Mexicans from Mexico.' But in the most politicized form, the Spanish ethos allowed Nuevomexicanos to lay claim to whiteness as an argument for full inclusion in the nation's body politic" (48–49).

Since whiteness historically depicts both power and privilege, the New Mexican Spanish identity was developed to distinctively isolate people so designated from being deemed as having a lesser racial value. By claiming whiteness as an identity, they are further denigrating all other raced groups in order to become more "whitened" versus being considered "blackened," but also aspiring to create an inroad for authentic group association. And most specifically, they drew a sharp line between black and nonblack, eliminating any notion of blackness as a feature of the Nuevomexicano mestizaje (Nieto-Phillips 2004). The anti-blackness of the United States created a situation where any acceptance of blackness in the Nuevomexicano identity would prevent New Mexico from becoming a state. Nativeness, while denigrated and demonized, was not treated with the same level of repulsion as blackness (Nieto-Phillips 2004).

An example of the how lighter skin is viewed as having social and political worth can be seen in an incident described by Logan. He explained that a mixed-raced, light-skinned faculty member at Cliff View College who identified as American Indian was viewed as having higher racial status. By allowing his skin complexion to become a form of status, Logan contended, this faculty member allowed himself to be used to assign darker-skinned American Indians less intellectual capital, and therefore less personal worth.

> There was a story that a faculty member told me . . . where he served on a lot of boards for Indigenous people. There were all kinds of representation but he was the fairest of the Native group. They would talk to him the most because he was light skinned. And this was a group of educated . . . you know . . . board-member type Native Americans, and because he was light skinned and spoke English a certain way . . . they just assumed that he was their leader. I just don't think that this type of stuff will necessarily go away, but he did not admit that he was not the leader.

Consciously or not, this faculty member participated in privileging whiteness by allowing himself to be viewed as more white and not the stereotype of an American Indian (poor language skills, brown complected, less educated, etc.). While others on the board allowed this to happen by bowing to this faculty member's racial and cultural capital, the faculty member could have done more to intervene in these racially privileging micro processes.

Another example is a fair-complexioned participant from northern New Mexico, Amy, who understood the advantages of "whiteness" and how her mixed-race identity choice could determine her social status. "I was always taught to be proud of who I was. So, maybe I even had a sense of, like, superiority . . . 'cause I'm Spanish, Native and white. 'Cause I guess they [whites] seem to have a sense of superiority." Although Amy acknowledges a mixed ancestry, her claim to whiteness has left her with the realization that she has a sense of racial superiority over those who have no claim to whiteness. This is not simply a personal issue for individuals like Amy. Claiming whiteness to gain advantage over others happens at a structural level and is, of course, nothing new. Self-labeling in New Mexico stems from relatively higher-status people wanting to be considered more Spanish than Mexican—that is, closer to white. Many have embraced the term *Hispanic* as a signifier that references a mostly European, or white, ancestry. The concept of "Hispanicness" is a group boundary marker that has been drawn, and it creates conflict between those who align their heritage with the people of Latin America rather than Spain—that is, Latino versus Hispanic. Less frequently, "some refuse both terms because both deny Indian ancestry" (Anzaldua 1999).

However, not everyone who claims Hispanic identity will do so consistently, which makes identity choice for some mixed-race students provisional and negotiable at Cliff View. Anthony explains, "Well, in Hawaii when I was going to school there, uhm . . . I always . . . I know I was Hispanic because my dad told me to be proud of it. But whenever I'd tell people, they'd say, 'Oh, you're from Mexico.' People don't understand that difference between Hispanics and Mexican . . . 'cause there is a very big . . . very big difference. . . . They always assume that I am white . . . always." The "one-drop rule" never applied to "Hispanicness"; instead class, race, and social status were the mixed complexities that were at play. But for New Mexican Hispanics with Native American heritage, the use of *Hispanic* versus *mestizo* suggests group alignment with Spanish lineage and a denouncement of, or at least a distancing from, American Indian heritage. As Anthony reasserts his identity as "Hispanic," he is working to lower the status of "Mexican," since it is understood to be less valued than Spanish heritage.

To further assert the comparison of Mexicanness versus Hispanicness in northern New Mexico, Amy, a light-skinned person of Spanish, American Indian, and white mixedness describes a point of view of Mexicanness.

> My best friend through junior high and high school was a boy named Tino. He was Mexican. He's very gangsterish, kinda thuggish . . . like "Don't tell me I'm Mexican [*laughs*] or I'll kick your ass." But he really was my best friend. He's a good guy for the most part. Hmm . . . we went all the way through together . . . all the way from like second grade to our senior year. But he would be so hurt if the Mexicans called him Mexican and he would be like, "I'm not Mexican!" But he clearly was Mexican . . . very dark skinned, short . . . you know he was. But he always says he was Spanish [*laughs*]. Like, I'm sorry, but Spanish people don't look like that.

By stating "Spanish people don't look like that," Amy is asserting and assigning a racial label, namely, that to be Mexican is to be phenotypically more American Indian. Thus, claiming Hispanic or Spanish identity is a way to mark boundaries and claim social distance above those who are less European and more Indigenous, in a racial sense. Since New Mexican Spanish identity has been constructed in conjunction with the need for high-status colonizers to attain and maintain whiteness and strict group memberships, this further highlights how one's identity choice is connected to the denigration of certain raced groups.

Just as blood has become a signifier for American Indian racial and cultural identity, as a nonwhite group identifying as white, or mostly white, the category of Hispanics prompts a resurgence of a racial ideology discourse that further embraces certain races as having material wealth and higher social position. It is also worth noting that not all Hispanics have access to the advantages of identifying as white. However, since there is a large group that identifies as white and Hispanic in New Mexico, this can be seen as a lens to expand the boundaries of "whiteness" for certain groups or members within a certain group, while continuing to disenfranchise other nonwhite raced groups.

## Advantages and Disadvantages: Mixed-Race Identity Choice

The disadvantages of being mixed race were easy to identify as the interviews and group sessions provided more information about family racial and cultural backgrounds and the influence of outside perceptions on students' daily experiences. Moreover, while some of the participants described how appearing white was a disadvantage, others detailed how appearing black resulted in more extensive social exclusion. Kathy felt her blackness has allowed her to see a lot more problems than other mixed-race people on campus. She viewed her experience as a mixed race person at Cliff View to be negative. "I feel that being mixed race is a disadvantage. I know I shouldn't say it, but that's the truth. Having heritages that contradict or are at odds with each other is an emotional and psychological mind game. Being a part of this and a part of that often leads a person to feel as if they are not really a member of anything. Divided loyalties and worldviews get in the way of being settled and balanced as a person. That is my experience." Tony saw his mixed-race background as providing a perspective of tense and confusing racial situations.

> You know . . . I always get the look. "What are you?" But most of the time people say things around me that are just crazy without even knowing my background. Having close relatives that could pass as white and my mother . . . I see it from all sides. Most people automatically assume I'm African American, but when they look at me up close . . . they look at my hair, and then you can imagine the questions going through their mind. And then my kids . . . they are half Dine and then they are really confused because they speak their traditional language. We get the looks, the stares . . . even on the reservation. My kids shouldn't have to experience that . . . it's crazy.

Both Kathy and Tony are "the same but different." As black-identified mixed-race people, they acknowledged that there was an obvious difference in how they are perceived on campus when compared to nonblack mixed-race people. Tony says,

> On campus or in class or anywhere, white is still viewed as being some sort of access. And to be mixed with white and have obvious white features . . . then they will have a different experience versus me. Hey, people off the bat because I'm brown say, "He must be African American but he doesn't quite fit the part." And in class, I'm often just totally disregarded, but a person that I know is mixed . . . it's obvious they are of mixed background and with white heritage . . . their input in class seems more important. It's as if it's okay for them to participate in the discussion but I don't fit the part . . . too non-Native looking.

Tony's experiences further support how blackness within a classroom setting at Cliff View College is viewed as having no inroad to "some sort of access" to an American Indian group association. Also, Tony's contributions to class discussions are viewed as being inauthentic based on his particular form of black-associated mixedness and phenotypic appearance.

Kathy has experienced a similar form of boundary demarcation. In her case, it arose in relation to her art. She describes how her blackness is used to exclude her from being seen as a legitimate producer of American Indian art.

> On this campus, there are few opportunities to practice and learn traditional arts. And most of my artwork and projects are engulfed in traditional arts . . . especially my beadwork. But because the information on my work states "non-enrolled tribal member of Eastern Band of Cherokees," people kind of question my knowledge and my connection to my Native American heritage. They obviously do not treat those that are mixed with white or appear phenotypically white the same . . . there is a different level of treatment. It has been hard being here because of the . . . disconnect and knowing that people do question me, but . . . my personality . . . keeps them at bay. They just don't know what I might say if they come across as just being ignorant. White mixed-race students on this campus are mostly not questioned as us brown mixed-race students. It's something that they need to address and openly have a dialogue about on campus. But so many people have been mistreated and shut down based on having an opinion that most students just deal with it.

Based on the 1990 Indian Arts and Crafts Act, Kathy cannot produce for profit traditional art labeled as American Indian because she is not enrolled in a American Indian tribe.[5] The issue of being an unenrolled tribal member places her in a status of being inauthentic in regard to her Indianness. But the larger picture is how a black mixedness has less value at Cliff View College than white mixedness. The value of whiteness as a symbolic factor of race is an inroad for the acceptance of artwork as American Indian if it is produced by mixed-race students with white and phenotypically light complexions. Black mixed-race participants such as Kathy and Tony are grouped as outsiders solely because they lack the phenotypic traits associated with an insider membership. As a result, their artwork is not viewed as legitimate American Indian art.

The oppressive structures that are at play are the social and political influences of being raced and how society has made whiteness a valuable norm. There is a significant racial issue at Cliff View College: Who controls the definition of cultural and traditional art? By and large, white supremacist ideology has determined how one is defined racially, in particular being American Indian through blood quantum. And the absence of discussion as to why lighter-skinned mixed-race students are not questioned about their Indianness to the degree that dark-skinned mixed-race students are opens up the reality that control over what counts as "Native" is as much a problem of "internal" racial politics as anything else. To hone in on the real problem, the issue is not just how to best define a cultural and traditional perspective; it is how to account for the historical and contemporary workings of race when it comes to notions of authenticity.

Moore's (2006) work supports the findings of this study. Based on her research of mixed-race schooling experiences, she asserts, "The student participants described how being monoracially labeled by others and categorized into a monoracial identity affected how students felt in school and how they defined themselves" (122). This means that mixed-race with black individuals are often forced to live within color boundaries created by the social construction of race. They are denied access to a nonblack identity, and thus to higher social status. In turn, a self-image is created by how others categorize them racially. Kathy's comment that "white mixed-race students on this campus are mostly not questioned as us brown mixed-race students" substantiates the color boundaries of the social and political race structures at Cliff View College.

Stacey, being a white/American Indian mixed-race person, was the only nonblack/American Indian mixed-race participant who viewed being mixed race as a disadvantage. Her feelings had a lot to do with her experiences with her father's family. "On my dad's side of the family I don't really feel accepted because, like . . . you know, they're white and you know, they like pick on us. I don't feel accepted by them. Awkward . . . it's an uncomfortable feeling around them. So it's hard like when you are mixed with different races and you want to be proud of all of them. But like when they aren't nice to you . . . you feel bad that you are a part of them." Stacey makes clear the pain of being denied acceptance based on phenotypic appearances by the gatekeepers of group membership in one's own family. It seems that Stacey's whiteness was not enough for her father's family, thus drawing distinctions between notions of "pure" and "tainted" whiteness.

Overall, most of the disadvantages described by the study participants in both groups occurred in relation to a person's skin tone. Similarly, the advantages described below occurred in the context of race-based colorism. Students, when asked about the benefits of being mixed race, answered almost unilaterally that they saw issues from many perspectives. Many of the participants expressed some sort of pride in being mixed race. They also believed that their mixedness gave them an ability to experience different group associations and appreciate other viewpoints. Amy and Anthony had similar outlooks on their mixedness. Amy felt her mixed-race status has been "a great opportunity to become well rounded in different cultures and just be me." Anthony cited his mixed-race identity as "an advantage because I feel like I get a unique perspective from different cultural groups, which is a beautiful thing." And he felt his mixed-race background provided him with a unique position. "People often just assume that I am white, but I'm Hispanic. But because I look white, I'm often judged different from the rest of my friends who look Native or Hispanic. I just feel coming from a background of different cultures versus just one . . . I have more to be proud of, and since I have been coming to this campus . . . it's definitely a big part to know your culture."

Anthony's perspective ignores the racial reality of privilege associated with phenotypically "looking white." His view that being "mixed" is a chance to float freely between and among various groups stands in stark contrast to those in this study who have been denied such an option. Lyda (2008) examined the factors that influence mixed-race self-identity, such as how one is perceived by others. Lyda puts into context the affect of phenotypic perceptions: "Phenotype can be both a social facilitator and/or barrier to racial group acceptance and affiliation. And as a result, phenotype can influence a multiracial student's self-identity, as well as the identity others (particularly monoracial others) project onto them, causing a racial socialization dialectic that can shape multiracial students' identity" (70). In other words, identity for a mixed-race person seems perpetually trapped in a dialectic between inclusion and exclusion, avowed and ascribed identities, in a system of racial schema. Skin tone often returns race discourse into a discussion based on phenotypic appearance and the realities that constructs for mixed-race people.

Although Logan has a brown complexion and phenotypically appears American Indian, he perceived his mixed-race background as an asset.

> You know . . . I have a close tie from both sides . . . Native and white. But I look Native and I'm fully accepted with no problems like some people might have experienced. My white side of the family have never treated me different or made me feel different because of my appearance. So, I've always felt like I belong. I can fit in and feel just as comfortable with my white side as much as my Native side. I don't mind being me and all that comes with me.

In addition, Logan believed his mixed-race background gave him an empathetic perspective on racial tension. He felt he understood the problems of those who identified as American Indian but did not have the phenotypic characteristics that would allow them to be accepted into group membership.

Samantha felt her identity gave her a different lens on "whiteness." Being mixed-race white and American Indian, she often felt her phenotypic features gave her more of an inroad experience to whiteness than someone who could not pass as white.

> Like most of the time . . . people just see me as white. So, I'm not always treated different. In class, they just assume that I'm smarter because of the way I look and speak. I don't have a problem in that way. I'm proud of my white heritage, too. Living in Farmington, New Mexico . . . it was just different for me than other Natives. No one was really mean to me and I know it's because often they just peg me as white or look at me as being white. Other Natives had problems but not me . . . so . . . it's kind of an advantage.

Like Samantha, Amy felt her phenotypic features gave her an advantage living in New Mexico.

> A lot of people just think I'm white, but they sure don't think I'm Mexican [*laughs*] and definitely not Native. My friends sometimes catch a lot of crap from other people because they are dark. That never happens to me. I wouldn't want to have to deal with that . . . I never have to deal with that. They just assume because I'm light skinned I'm okay, but if you are dark . . . that's not okay. Being brown here can sometimes . . . cause problems for you. Look at me . . . I look white . . . so . . . it's just different for me.

The comments of students who viewed their mixed-race as an advantage—"That never happens to me," "I'm not always treated different," or "People just assume I'm white"—meant that they are acknowledging the power structures that position whiteness as a symbol of authority and that place less worth on nonwhite races. Often these structures played out in varying discourses with the students. Their situation becomes problematic when a particular discourse places them in a position of participating in asserting privilege over other nonblack mixed-raced people. This stance provides them with racial prosperity, while simultaneously allowing them to ignore that others will be left to stand alone against racial inequality.

Mixed-race students' self perceptions were heavily influenced by their lived experiences. Conversations that took place around their elementary and secondary experiences were recounted at the collegiate level. College presented a new setting in which some students participated in negotiating their identity choice, while others were assigned a racial label. In this process most students had a choice about their identity, whereas some students—namely, black/American Indian mixed-race participants—were assigned to one race and accepted a monoracial status as a way to survive at Cliff View. Those students that were assigned to one race—that is, black—experienced alienation from the larger American Indian ethnoracial group association.

Identity for many mixed-raced students began with negotiated assertions, or an ongoing process of assertion and "action-reaction." Their experiences are multiple and various, filled with many different personal stories and interpretations that often shift based on their evolving process of understanding the social meaning of race.

## Notes

1. "Mexican" denotes a person of mixed Spanish and American Indian descent.

2. "Colorism embodies preference and desire for both light skin and as well as these other attendant features. Hair, eye color, and facial features function along with color in complex ways to shape opportunities, norms regarding attractiveness, self-concept, and overall body image" (Thompson and Keith 2001, 338).

3. The Indian Reorganization Act of 1934, also known as the Wheeler-Howard Act or, informally, the Indian New Deal, was US federal legislation that secured certain rights for American Indians and Alaskan Natives. These included the reversal of the Dawes Act's privatization of common holdings of American Indians and a

return to local self-government for tribal bases. The act also restored to American Indians the management of their assets (mainly land) and included provisions intended to make sound economic foundations for the inhabitants of Indian reservations.

The Oklahoma Indian Welfare Act, also known as the Thomas-Rogers Act, extended the Indian Reorganization Act of 1934. It sought to return some form of tribal government to many tribes in formal Indian Territory.

4. "Hispanic" denotes a US citizen of Latin American or Spanish descent. "mestizo" denotes a person of mixed racial ancestry, especially mixed European and American Indian ancestry.

5. The Indian Arts and Crafts Act of 1990 (P.L. 101-644) is a truth-in-advertising law that prohibits misrepresentation in marketing of [American] Indian arts and crafts products within the United States. It is illegal to offer or display for sale, or sell any art or craft product in a manner that falsely suggests it is Indian produced, an Indian product, or the product of a particular [American] Indian or [American] Indian Tribe or [American] Indian arts and crafts organization, resident within the United States. An [American] Indian is defined as a member of any federally or State recognized [American] Indian Tribe, or an individual certified as an [American] Indian artisan by an [American] Indian Tribe.

# 5

## Peer Interactions
## and Influences

Through students' stories about their interactions with other racial communities, one is able to glean the racial assumptions and misconceptions that shape racial interactions. Most often the response to and interaction among mixed-race students and others depends upon the mixed-race student's appearance. In a related vein, a common experience among those with discernible differences was responding to racial judgments or a questioning of their Indianness. Acceptance or rejection from their peers often seemed to be associated with the crowd with which mixed-race students connected. It is clear that initial interactions were based almost exclusively on visible appearance.

## Perceivable Differences

Pulera (2002) focused an entire book on the racial implications of perceived phenotypic differences and concluded: "Observable differences in physical appearance separating the races are the single most important factor shaping intergroup relations, in conjunction with the social, cultural, economic, and

DOI: 10.5876/9781607325444.c005

political ramifications that accompany this visual divide. These dynamics animate the unceasing struggles for power, recognition, and resources that occur
between, among, and within American racial groups" (8–9). Many students
in this study shared stories that revealed how the frequent desires for racial
openness and noncategorization cause friction vis à vis the real politics of
everyday life in a white supremacist society. An important factor to consider is
how a racial caste system constructs different versions of reality for nonblack
and black mixed-race people. In other words, the existence of racial castes
have ontological and epistemological implications for mixed-race people.
Most nonblack mixed-race people view multiracial reality as having a variety
of fluid options to more successfully navigate pro-white realms. On one hand,
such belief creates a fundamental position that does not critique the biological and political construction of race. On the other, black mixed-race people
are placed in more alienated positions. As a result, mixed-race groups with
dark phenotypic features become suspicious of lighter mixed-race people
who seek a higher-status group association. The racial reality is that mixed-
race people with certain phenotypic features, that is, "whiter" and/or more
European looking, are assigned more human value and reap more material
and psychic reward. This discursive and material practice of assigning value is
based on certain mixed-race unions having a specific status embedded in the
existing rankings and inequalities of a white supremacist racial order.

For example, as a fair-complected nonblack mixed-race person, Samantha
experienced group exclusion from her mixed-race American Indian peers.

> In my experience, the only thing that influenced my racial identity was who
> surrounded me. First, I started off surrounded by Navajos. So, naturally I felt
> like the whitest person around because of my light skin. Then, our family
> moved to Farmington, New Mexico and was surrounded by a mix of whites
> and Natives. When I hung out with white people at school, I felt Native
> and when I hung out with the Natives, I felt white. And at school . . . for
> instance, we would have lunch tables . . . you know. And . . . all of the white-
> complexioned students were friends and we tried to talk to other students,
> like try to hang out and play basketball. But . . . even on the basketball
> court . . . they would pass it to their friends who were not like white look-
> ing . . . you know. And it wasn't because we were white looking . . . I mean we
> were all half-breeds but they just chose us because we more light complexioned.

Samantha's group authenticity was questioned based on her light skin. And due to the political nature of skin color having both a material and political value, a white / American Indian mixed-race person who phenotypically appears white is questioned because there is a long history of those who use their light skin color as an advantage in order to become upwardly mobile, or at least to be less denigrated. After all, white people are more comfortable with those whom they think look like them.

Amy's experience was similar to Samantha's. It included direct questioning of her identity by her peers. "Because like I look white . . . I get questioned by people on campus. You know, like, 'Are you Native? What percent are you? How much?' I was like, 'Why are they asking me all of these questions? They don't know me.'" Amy's experience with American Indian group boundary marking is yet another example of how skin color is seen a political leverage. Anthony gives a candid perspective of why peers judge one another. "I believe issues arise from students when they feel that they need to prove themselves to the rest because they feel deep down that others are going to judge them. From my experiences with peers, this type of attitude arises from light-skinned Natives who feel that they won't be recognized as Native by their darker-complexioned brothers and sisters." Unlike Anthony's recognition that many American Indians will not trust those mixed-race members who look white, Samantha's and Amy's discourses do not convey an acknowledgment of the power structures that are at play, nor do they acknowledge that "looking white" gives them a status position within a racial hierarchy.

The history of white advantage positions many light-skinned multiracials as "posers," or intruders on the terrain of authenticity. Logan, a brown-complected mixed-race person, discussed his problem with some light-skinned mixed-race peers. "I find it annoying when people who lack a connection with their culture go into society and do nothing to further the positive image of that culture. For example, when a light-skinned multiracial individual goes into town and, in an attempt to be trendy and cool, strikes up a conversation that doesn't shine in a positive light on their cultural community, that bothers me. They are so desperate just so they can fit in." These actions by lighter-skinned American Indians create consequences for the disenfranchised group and divisions that lead to automatic suspicion of the lighter-complected mixed-race person as someone who will distort the image of American Indian people.

Logan openly discussed a conversation with his college roommate that gave a clear indication of how cultural styles also evoke notions of American Indian ethnoracial authenticity.

> There was a new girl touring the campus, and my roommate is all the time talking about women. He was like, "Man, she was really pretty. Unfortunately, she's got a man with her . . . another one of those thugs." And he said, "Don't you think that's sad?" I was like, "What do you mean?" He said, "It's stupid to see Natives dressed all up in G-Unit clothing and walking around all gangster." I was like, "I'm not sure what you mean." And he was like, "Why are they trying to be black?" Well, the hip-hop culture is not necessarily black culture, I mean it's more than that now. And he said, "Well, you know what I mean. They are acting all thuggish and hard." I was like . . . "Maybe because they are."

Logan's roommate's depiction of "thuggish" as a stereotypical portrait of black culture creates an image that the majority of the black population are members of gangs and commit illegal acts as a norm of daily behavior. It also draws a line of social distinction between blacks and American Indians: one thuggish, one not.

Although Logan was very opinionated about a peer stereotyping someone as being "thuggish," and thus not American Indian enough, in a later conversation he categorized someone as "playing Indian." Logan's views often changed based on the social and political situation or the context of the discourse. For example, he said the following:

> Anyway, the point I'm trying to make is that he is claiming his heritage [so] as to [become] . . . a poster child. He's [Sam Bradford] one-sixteenth Cherokee. I mean, he will go down in history as the first Native American Heisman winner, which I think is a hurray for Native American[s]. But then you've got Jim Thorpe, Johnny Bench . . . you've got all kinds of great athletes who are now going to be underneath him as far as history remembers . . . because he has the highest honor in college football and it's a story tradition. Yeah . . . his claim to fame . . . now all of a sudden he's Native . . . that's just ridiculous.

Logan's willingness to define a person's authenticity reiterates the racialized political nature of group association.

Demarcations of group boundaries play out in how people organize themselves in social space. Group associations, though personal on one level, take on larger social meaning. For instance, Kim and Stacey experienced situations at Cliff View where groups of peers sit together in the cafeteria based on their constructed sense of authentic Indianness. Kim viewed the cafeteria as a place where people separated themselves.

> In the cafeteria . . . I noticed that only certain students sit together and when you walk by some of them kinda laugh. They just look at you like you are crazy because you don't look like them . . . it's weird. So . . . I usually just take my lunch to go. You have the darker Natives at this table and the light-skinned people over here. They just look at you as if you don't fit into whatever group, as if you are an alien. People around here just don't get it . . . we are all the same. But . . . I guess not to them . . . maybe I'm not dark enough or too brown to sit at the other tables.

And since authenticity defines group association, it is not uncommon for darker-skinned American Indians to be leery of lighter-skinned American Indians, who receive more advantages in a white supremacist system. In regard to societal influences, the final determination of group association in many cases is how you align yourself both socially and politically within a racialized power structure. So, lighter skin is viewed as providing an inroad to less discrimination, therefore, darker-skinned people will view lighter-skinned people as actively not aligning themselves with denigrated groups, distancing themselves from those with lower status, thus helping to reify status differences.

Stacey's views of the cafeteria groupings are similar to Kim's.

> Like . . . you know . . . you walk in and you see that everyone is just divided. Some people are like over here in this group and other people are like . . . just hanging out. I don't have a problem with anyone on campus, but yeah . . . some students just sit together . . . and like I notice it's the darker Natives that always seems to hang out with just that group. But I'm cool with everyone. Yeah . . . the white Natives hang out together a lot on campus and they dress the same. I don't know why but they do. I don't like hanging out in the cafeteria . . . bad vibes.

Stacey's views of "bad vibes" pinpoint the politics of skin color at Cliff View and the group associations of certain mixedness on campus that are comparable to the larger societal influences of group membership. It is interesting to experience what is essentially racial segregation at what is supposedly a monoracial, that is, "Native," school. It is worth noting that since the cafeteria is a facet of Cliff View College's social realm, it reflects the values and attitudes of the broader societal norms of whiteness that in turn impact students' schooling experiences.

Kathy has faced reactions from peers, particularly at Cliff View, about her appearance. While a number of nonblack/American Indian participants could fit into some kind of group association within an American Indian community based on their cultural and traditional knowledge, Kathy lacked both cultural and phenotypic similarities to her peers. Kathy's experiences seem to have been similar throughout her school years, according to her account of her younger years as a mixed-race person. "When I was in the ninth grade, I expressed myself as a black girl. I went to school on an army base with kids from around the world, but my track teammates were primarily black and white. As hard as I tried to fit in with the black kids, they always called me out and exposed my mixed heritage. I can't pass for anything other than a mutt." Kathy gives another example of being raced by a peer, who categorizes who he thinks can or should identify as an American Indian artist.

> For instance, there is this guy in one of my classes and he's . . . you know . . . he's a mixed guy . . . he's a Native mixed with French. And . . . when we have discussions based on blood quantum or in this particular case it was about the art market and about the . . . laws governing who can or who's Indian or who can be in it and whatnot. He was very . . . aggressive . . . you could say that with his opinions . . . you know, about the keeping people out and everything. . . . And by the same token . . . when he's around me and we are having critiques in art classes and things like that . . . he's very opinionated of my work . . . so, it's like he views me as I can't participate in this or that. He just beats people up all the time with the Indian art stuff and who's Indian enough to participate.

A different example of Kathy's art being criticized by her peers includes the topic of mixed race.

> I worked on a project about how different groups express their identity in their art differently. And that's what my project was about and the person . . . I was interviewed for the gallery show. My family . . . they were Cherokees. And it

incorporates the artwork that I do. Well . . . after the opening . . . I guess they
[my peers] were like . . . they were saying things like, "Why does she always
have to be doing the work on this . . . why does she always have to bring this
up?" So, it was a very frustrating experience to always have with peers.

As a result of Kathy being mixed race with black, more than often her experiences have included the questioning of her group association and the authenticity of her Indianness.

Tony recognizes the criticisms of peers but also provides an insight into
the practice of racial demarcations at Cliff View, such as how colorism influences where students sit in the cafeteria.

Some of the students would just rather stick together. There is often tension
between who is viewed more "Native" than the other. You know, some of the
students from the rez just don't get it. They sometimes just give you the look
and that look is "Oh, so you think you are Native. Do you live on the rez?" So,
I think a lot of the younger students or students that look a certain way are
intimidated by those "looks" and just sit with people they have similarities
with. Now who would have ever thought that a bunch of Natives would
do this to one another? Times haven't changed much. But in the cafeteria,
you would think that students would relax more . . . talk about whatever.
Socializing on this campus is just difficult at times . . . it's just different.

Tony's experiences bring to mind the idea of being generically American
Indian, and in this case, the definition of "Indian" would depend on which
group of students you were to ask in the Cliff View cafeteria. That certain
groups sit together is an example of how racialized group membership, or Indianness, is formed and re-formed.

Mixed-race students' perceivable differences were associated with their
experiences of either acceptance or rejection from their peers. Inclusion
or exclusion was conducted through tests of authentic versus inauthentic
Indianness. Other contributing factors to this placement on one side of the
line or the other included what race each student seemed to identify with
most closely (phenotypically, socially, and politically). When a student's
mixedness (i.e., white or black mixedness) was obvious, such as mixed race
with white and phenotypically white features, many students either negotiated within the white realms of privilege or perceived themselves as victims,

denied full inclusion. In contrast, those with black mixedness continued to experience substantial disenfranchisement and alienation, marked primarily as outsiders. In the focus group, reactions to these experiences varied among students, with some being more empathetic than others. Unfortunately, students did not decide to organize or seek out peer groups, but their experiences did shape the students' self-identity and perceptions of others. Moreover, Cliff View College, as an educational institution, did not operate outside of racialized societal norms and therefore facilitated the racial ordering of students (as seen in the cafeteria). As a result, some students viewed Cliff View College as hindering their artistic and academic experiences based on their phenotypic mixedness.

## Surviving the Losses

There is obviously a familial impact on how Indianness is defined, renegotiated, and asserted, but there is also an overall sense of identity survival among peers. As described by Paul Ongtooguk (as cited in Tatum 1997), an Alaskan Native educator,

> It seemed remarkable to me, as an adolescent boy, that anybody had survived in that community let alone found a way to sustain a distinctive way of life and maintain a rich and complex culture. I realized then that here were members of Alaskan Native community who were working to create the conditions in which all could have lives with dignity and be well regarded as human beings. This realization was the result of becoming acquainted with Alaskan Native leaders working in the community with Native elders trying to preserve the legacy of our society and introduce the young people to that legacy. (151)

There is a sense of survival among American Indian people. As a result, group membership through peer interaction is often a symbol of identity, especially at Cliff View College. Through "surviving the losses," many peer interactions result in long-term relationships and often are encouraged by family members.

Stacey's family has always encouraged an American Indian identity. They hope that by attending a tribal college, she will meet an American Indian companion to continue her family's legacy of survival.

Yeah . . . my family has always wanted me to marry a Native guy, and to
be honest, I would prefer keeping it Native. Like most people just don't
understand . . . it's different. It's important to keep my bloodline going and
kids would be awesome! Older people that went to boarding schools talked
about meeting their husbands or wives there . . . and it didn't matter what
tribe . . . they were just Native. They were just surviving . . . like it's just doing
your part . . . you know?

Stacey's family supports and influences her views on the importance of having a racially American Indian partner.

Logan's views of survival are similar to Stacey's. "When you really think
about it, the fate of my family lies in blood quantum . . . unfortunately. And
if I marry a non-Native, my children's blood quantum becomes even lower
since I'm only half. I would prefer to be a Native person . . . my girlfriend is
Native and I met her here. Is she a member of my tribe? No, but she's Native
regardless." As Logan explained, since there is a sense of survival among students at Cliff View College (regarding, for example, blood quantum enrollment policies), many of the participants explicitly stated their racial preference for an American Indian partner. Amy candidly explained, "My mom has
always embraced our Native culture and especially the idea of me being at
Cliff View College . . . you know . . . being around other Natives. She came
here as a student, too. And if I was going to be in a relationship with someone . . . they would be Native. We make friends here and sometimes that
turns into dating . . . I have always liked Native guys." Amy also has a sense
of survival through partnership. The desire for a "Native" partner seems premised on the notion that race is in fact a biological essence, regardless of
notions about Nativeness being a mostly cultural phenomenon.

Anthony had a perspective of cultural survival rather than racial survival
being supported at Cliff View College:

Not until I came to this school did I really start to think about my heritage.
It just seems that everyone is so into who they are or learning more about
themselves that know[ing] about your culture and traditional heritage is really
a plus. Like hanging around my best friend, who is Native from Taos, has
taught me to be proud of all my parts. And being on campus, I have really felt
like I need to learn more about me and who I am. It's so important here on
campus and with my friends that I want to learn more, so that I know truly

who I am. Not just as a gay guy that looks white, but really all my parts and my culture. It's important and here . . . I feel such a push for us to know more and it's supported to do that. For me, it's just what I need.

And since group association and authenticity are also connected to cultural knowledge, Anthony described the importance of being "proud of all my parts."

Kathy bluntly stated that her racial preference for a partner was "Native American men . . . I have my preferences . . . me and my friends call them the brown boys." However, Tony had a perspective of cultural and traditional survival rather than racial survival.

> Being married to a Dine woman and having children together, it is so important for my children to carry on her traditions . . . you keep it alive. Yeah . . . my kids are mixed with what I bring to the plate, but my wife has brought them up in her culture and traditions. And I'm okay with that . . . I'm supportive. But I'm supportive of who they want to be with . . . marry or whatever, but being in an environment where they can share their culture and traditions with someone like them is also important. All of my children speak their language and hopefully, so will my grandchild. Being Dine to my family is so important and being with someone that can relate to that would be great for them. You know, life is so hard on people that are not white, and it's important that they remember that and have someone they can relate to. Being on campus . . . regardless of my experience, students can have an outlet . . . it's important to find a balance. I just wish the best for my kids. And if my son does choose to come back to college here . . . he can bring his family and still do what he needs to do.

Tony explains that Cliff View College supports "surviving the losses" through family housing and with future goals of opening a daycare center on campus. Such provisions show that American Indian self-determination has evolved into a need to stem the tide of the multigenerational losses of many American Indian communities through a lens of a governmentally determined blood quantum and biological essence—that is, maintaining the "race" is at least as important as maintaining the "culture." And with self-determination goes a focus on survival, and thus the major issue becomes how to survive governmental determination in a tribal college learning environment while remaining American Indian against the odds. Cliff View, as a matter of policy, provides the infrastructure to perpetuate the creation of children who "look" Native. While this is in a way a form of survival, it is also a way to reify the boundaries of who counts racially as an American Indian person.

An analysis of the students' discourse on survival highlights two points of view. One stance is the perspective of racial survival. On the other hand, there is a stance of cultural and traditional survival. Because race is used as a device to categorize people based on the power structures of whiteness, the need to racially survive based on blood quantum will further assert and assign racial labels. More important, it will widen the gap between acknowledged and nonacknowledged members to group association as American Indian. As blood quantum continues to play a role in the woven fabric of tribal enrollment and access to economic resources, the divisions between different mixed groups will heighten the strife of race dynamics. In this way, blood quantum, once internalized, operates as a wedge within Native people, drawing status distinctions and lines of membership.

There is much reason to believe that the notion of blood quantum has already been normalized. Logan provides keen insight into the naturalization of blood quantum discourse at Cliff View College, supplying an example of racial dynamics that divide students into insider versus outsider group associations.

> We were doing a project in class . . . so the instructor brought in professors from all different walks of life and one of them mentioned how . . . it's weird how the Native community is the only community where outsiders feel like it is okay to question their Nativeness or their race. You know, essentially like . . . there was a panel after a film about Native sovereignty or something and an audience member . . . which was a student on this campus . . . asked the panelists if they were full blood. We also had two guest writers come to class and again . . . one of our students on campus asked them if they were full blood. And I looked at my teacher and I said, "Oh my God." Because you know, not only does this happen from outsiders but also it happens from insiders. But for students on this campus to question if someone is full blood is just re-creating a stereotype of who is worthy of saying that they are Indian and who is not.

Logan makes a powerful point—what other ethnoracial group subjects itself so openly to questions about racial biological lineage? And while it can be argued that American Indian people have little choice in that matter because the US government is the driving force behind blood quantum, there is also an element of complicity. What makes blood quantum so enticing is that it is a way to dole out relative power and privilege within the American Indian community. This is done not only by the government but also by American Indian people themselves, in part, through the practice of colorism and inter-ethnic racism.

If a person is not allowed into group membership based on not having the appropriate blood quantum value or phenotypic features, raced people with accepted group membership are indeed active participants of a racial hierarchy. For example, the concept of American Indian group membership being determined by blood quantum dictates a person's access to cultural and traditional practices that often define one's tribal connection and group association as an insider versus an outsider. And in certain situations, one's mixedness determines if group membership will hold a certain value. Blood quantum directly impacts the myth of tribal sovereignty and reaffirms the realities of the power structures that uphold raced categories. Neither the politics of blood quantum nor the myth of tribal sovereignty can create immunity for a raced group from the social and political power structures of a white supremacist legacy, particularly under government policies and laws. As governmental decrees determined the blood quantum of blacks as being the "one-drop" rule, the same power dynamics are at play to determine tribal membership or recognition.

As blood quantum becomes the deciding factor for authenticity of one's Indianness, the power structures at play will then determine the nonexistence of Indianness as more tribal communities are becoming generationally mixed raced. The overarching issue is to dismiss white social and political structures, while decolonizing the construction of the desire to attain whiteness. This will be difficult to do when the internal structure of American Indian communities are stratified by colorism.

We turn now to addressing mixed-race students' representations of the impact of multiraciality on their academic experiences. I will look specifically at the role of the push for American Indian self-determination at Cliff View. Also, I will consider the reasons why these mixed-race students chose to attend a tribal college.

# 6

## The Impact of Race on
## Academic Experiences

Students had few if any positive things to say about how Cliff View College addressed their needs as a mixed-race American Indian population. Rather, they described being placed by the college into identifiable raced groups and being addressed in that context for the remainder of their college careers. Being placed according to a specific affiliation (Certificate of Indian Blood, federally or nonfederally recognized tribe, "Indianness," etc.) was reassuring for some students but caused anxiety for others. Students described the process of asserting, assigning, or renegotiating their identity based on how their mixedness is perceived and how such a process created an action-reaction identity choice. As a backdrop for the role Cliff View played in asserting, assigning, or renegotiating mixed race Indianness, I will first discuss the legacy of "educating the Indian" together with the role of tribal colleges. I will then describe mixed-race students' reactions to the tribal college environment at Cliff View and the impact on academic experiences within this institutional setting.

DOI: 10.5876/9781607325444.c006

## Role of Tribal Colleges

For more than a century, the US government worked to "educate the Indian" and end poverty on reservations. As Deloria (1999) so precisely stated, "Educating the Indians to truth, be it religious, economic, or scientific, was regarded as the duty of the civilized man" (159). A few efforts were well intentioned, but many only exacerbated the effects of postcolonialism. From the mid-1800s to the late 1900s, American Indians remained among the poorest of the poor. Located in some of the most isolated corners of the country, reservations have often felt more like Third World nations.

Visible now through the legacy of failed federal policies such as boarding schools trying to instill a work ethic based on whiteness are many stories of the brutality of lost identity, lost language, and "lost generations" that resulted from "educating the Indian." In hindsight, there were multiple reasons for governmental failure. For example, the belief that American Indian culture and tribal values needed to be assimilated into mainstream white American culture often resulted in the use of force. The government believed that elders and leaders should be treated like children until they were capable of functioning under societal norms based on white power and privilege.

Assimilation produced various forms of resistance, one of which grew into a powerful political movement during the 1960s. A new generation of tribal leaders coalesced around a policy of tribal "self-determination," which gained support from President Lyndon Johnson in 1968. One of the most profound acts motivated by the notion of self-determination was the founding of tribally controlled colleges, chartered by tribes and governed by American Indians. Tribal colleges were the first institutions to fully integrate tribal culture and values into their mission statements and day-to-day work. In this new era, tribal colleges believe they must train leaders as well as workers, while providing opportunities for American Indian students to learn about their past, study their language, and practice their ceremonies with pride and a sense of purpose. Today, there are thirty-six tribal colleges, and they will continue to evolve as the self-determination movement matures.

## Schooling Experiences

Reflecting on the broader context of social and political inequalities, Critical Race Theory can be used as a probe to understand the complexities of law, racial ideology, and political power contributing to the postcolonial effects of "educating the Indian" and how such effects are lived experiences at a tribal college for mixed-race students. The passing of the Indian Education Act in 1972 promised to provide adequate and appropriate educational services for American Indians.[1] The act represented a major initiative toward rectifying the cataclysmic effects of centuries of mistreatment and abuse. While Cliff View College is a product of this act, and thus of the larger notion of self-determination, a number of mixed-race students spoke about how their college experiences were not what they anticipated. In some instances, they felt the college painted an inaccurate picture of what to expect, such as the image of a learning environment where all American Indians regardless of their blood quantum or phenotypic features would feel safe from having to renegotiate their identity or justify their authenticity as a result of their particular form of race mixedness.

When participants were asked why they chose to attend a tribal college as a mixed-race person, some participants who brought up issues of their Indianness also expressed having a "need" to be around other American Indians. Students were asked about their learning experience and how they are viewed at Cliff View College as mixed-race students. Overall, there were varying responses based on their mixedness and their reaction to being raced.

Kathy and Tony are older students with earned degrees who have often been racially positioned as black based on their phenotypic features. Nonetheless, they had different reasons for attending a tribal college. Kathy explained,

> It was local and the reason I chose a tribal college over a community college is because I wanted to be around more Native people. It was that time . . . I needed to be around more Native people. It was something in me at that point that said that I needed to just be around more Natives . . . it's time. . . . I knew I just wanted to study more about my culture . . . about Natives. I had always looked at this one school for years, while I was in the navy. And I thought . . . wow . . . they are really doing cool art stuff . . . I did not know I wanted to be an artist, but I wanted to learn more about carving and some traditional arts. It was an automatic given. I need it . . . like I said . . . it was time.

Kathy's statement of "I needed to just be around more Natives" shows her desire to become associated with an American Indian identity. Being mixed race with black and having childhood memories of her family not acknowledging their American Indian lineage, Kathy's decision arose from a need to belong.

For Tony, family connections were influential in bringing him to Cliff View.

> Uhm . . . for me it was different . . . it was kinda not my choice . . . I was drawn to it. And what I mean by that is . . . I found out about the college years ago. And I have a lot of in-law relatives that went here and I had two friends that went here. And it was kinda through those relationships that kinda drew me here. Uhm . . . I established a relationship with a well-known Native artist . . . even prior to coming here. So, it was basically those relationships and ultimately when my kid started coming here . . . it drew me more to this area. My wife is Navajo and she is from this area, so it was like . . . when we decided to move back . . . the opportunity presented itself. And just in general being who I am, acknowledging my Native side . . . I thought it would be an added value and an opportunity to share as well as learn other cultures and my own . . . so. That's what kinda drew me here.

Although both Kathy's and Tony's reasons for attending Cliff View College were to learn more about their culture as well as others', Kathy's motive was based more on an effort to reclaim her authenticity through the study of cultural and traditional art forms. And since in most of both students' mixed-race experiences, they have been racialized, alienated, and viewed as outsiders based on their phenotypic features, their coming to Cliff View can be seen as an attempt to re-create a group association, to become more American Indian. Even so, "being drawn" or "needing" to experience Nativeness only further subjected both Kathy and Tony to the racial power dynamics that construct a higher-status multiracial reality for some and a lower-status monoracial reality for those deemed black.

In view of the fact that stereotypes are often assigned and played out, tribal colleges are often pegged with the mission of teaching students how to be "Indian." Jennifer's reason for attending a tribal college was not to re-create, renegotiate, or assert her identity.

> Just throwing it out there . . . just assuming we are an intertribal Native school and that we are all intertribal Natives. We all have our own creation stories . . . we all have our own traditions. We all have our own . . . whatever . . . I did not come to this school to learn how to build a teepee. Sometimes I hear

. . . [other students'] frustration of how other people are viewing them. And uhm . . . how they want to fit in a Native college environment and how they feel it's not working. People asking them questions about their blood quantum and stuff like that. And . . . I feel they have to prove how Indian they are. And . . . I just . . . if people don't believe me . . . that's too bad. I just be myself but I don't have to carry a feather in my pocket or anything [*laughs*]. The reason I feel the way I do is because I have to work so hard . . . to keep it important in my life because my family does not accept it.

For students who are mixed race with black, their experiences continued to be racialized through notions of questioning their authenticity of Indianness. For example, Tony describes how he is disregarded in classroom discussions by faculty at Cliff View College: "Instructors on this campus . . . literally have discounted . . . my comments or feedback in classroom discussions that were open forum because I don't appear to look Native or maybe I look African American or maybe a combination of neither. Based on their perspectives or . . . maybe they feel threatened . . . who knows." When Tony is disregarded in classroom discussions, the meaning of race becomes both a collective action and a personal practice by the gatekeepers of the discussion. In this process, Tony's blackness is shaped by racial meanings with specific rules that emerged as a product of white racism. More important, the gatekeepers of the dialogue are creating an oppressive learning environment based on students' phenotypic features and singularly asserting that blackness is inferior, or at least seemingly forever an outsider to Nativeness.

Relating a comparable but different experience, Kathy frankly portrays her familiarity with exclusion as a nonenrolled tribal member on campus.

There was a student activity going on during Indian market where some of the students were going to be able to set up booths and tables in front of the Cliff View College museum . . . to show their work. And originally the application for that stated that you had to have a CIB [Certification of Indian Blood] in order to participate. Well, I'm not the only student on this campus that doesn't have a CIB, but I felt like here I am being shunned out of something as a student of this school. I should be able to participate, so I already had a negative view of Indian market. I don't know what hoops they jumped through, but some of the other students [without a CIB] were allowed to participate. There have been things like that during my entire academic career here on campus. But now I feel like I'm a total outsider having to fight to get into something and . . . that could really impact my career in the future and my career choices. There are other things like . . . some staff were very hesitant or even resistant actually when they spoke with me when I would come in for whatever service that I needed and they would be very standoffish. How could I put this? I never really experienced this growing up, but you hear stereotypes about like a black person walking down a predominantly white street and they're pulling their kids to them or grabbing their purses . . . because they are like . . . oh my God they are going to steal something . . . it was almost that sort of feeling. That I read off certain individuals . . . not from students . . . like I said . . . these people that work here and . . . they were Natives.

Another encounter Kathy had pertained to a course project. She was very direct in describing her frustration during and after the experience.

There was an incident yesterday in class where . . . for drawing we had to create a vignette . . . make a form . . . to draw and it was using a pillowcase. And it was to be tied up by a rope and . . . hung from an easel. And that was what I needed to draw . . . worked on that four days. And the group that I was in . . . an individual created a noose out of the thick rope . . . and put it on the pillowcase and used it to be hung. And I sat there for twenty minutes in class trying to stare at this noose and this thing hanging from it and draw it. And I just could not . . . so I left the classroom angry. And I had to explain to the instructor as a person of color that was [a] very offensive symbol to me . . . it symbolized hate and . . . I really just did not want to have to look at. But she was like, "Why does it do these things?" She did not understand. And they did not understand, whether it be the historical or cultural or whatever reference behind this symbol, and why a person with black heritage would be offended by it.

Although Kathy embraces both her American Indian and black identities, the lack of cultural sensitivity to the done to violence of descendants of slaves in a classroom assignment further portrays the boundaries of being mixed race with black versus white.

Troy shared a similar experience of discomfort regarding a conversation among students on campus. "Students were making comments about race and were not being sensitive about what was being said. Being in ear distance, they were making comments about certain mixed-race students as if they could not hear them . . . it was so ignorant. Does it really matter how a person looks on this campus? And I would reply that it does change your experience . . . it sure does."

Other frustrations included the lowering of academic expectations. Kathy described her disappointment with the academic expectations at Cliff View College in comparison to nontribal colleges.

> Uhm . . . there are students at this school that I have no idea how in the world they are still allowed to come to campus. They miss half of the semester, but because they are from X, Y, Z tribe and maybe that tribe funnels a lot of money to the college . . . I don't know. I'm just putting it out there. These people are allowed to bounce and float in and out. There was a student who was in one of my classes that would come to class routinely an hour and half late . . . The instructor would stop and bring the student up to speed. Things like that would not be accepted at a predominantly white college or even a predominantly black college. So, I think that there is definitely a different standard here. Those particular students here should not be just passed along. That mentality of holding Johnny's hand and move him along because we need the numbers or whatever the case may be . . . that's doing a disservice to that student.

Jennifer's view was similar.

> The problem is that they are lowering expectations for certain races because they feel like they won't accomplish anything. I thought it was going to be harder when I came here and I've noticed that instructors here seem to feel that if they higher their expectations that the students will not have any hope to succeed. Students turn in papers and work late all the time . . . the same papers we did and we turn them in on time and they get the same grade that we do. That's just ridiculous . . . it's not fair.

The issue of having to prove your worth at Cliff View College continues to uphold how racial labels as are used as strategic essentialist tools. For example, Kathy's schooling experience has taught her that

> I will always be suspect and questioned by those I encounter. I will always have to prove my worthiness, cultural expertise and right to claim my heritage, in every aspect of my life. The racial climate on campus is one [I am] forced

to tolerate. There are obviously held racial or tribal biases, especially people that look like me. One faculty member told me, while I was wearing a scarf around my head, "You look more Indian now when you wear a bandana." I was shocked and angry that she would feel as if she had the right to tell me that it was only after I put on a scarf that I became Native in her eyes.

And through the use of strategic essentialist tools, faculty at Cliff View College are making a politically racialized choice on how they view color boundaries within already recognized raced groups.

In contrast to the black/American Indian mixed-race participants in this study, Samantha did not express the need to be around more American Indian people as a basis for her decision to attend a tribal college. For her, it mattered more that Cliff View was known for its art program.

I really didn't take the factor that this was a Native school because actually, to be honest . . . before I even came here . . . I knew that there were a lot of Native students. So, to me it was just like I wanted to get my art degree. I didn't want to think about it like what type of race the school was as long as I did what I wanted to. I really don't think that it should be a factor. You know . . . so when you are choosing school . . . it's like . . . if it's what you want to do. I think that's more important so.

It is interesting that race mattered so little for Samantha, a light-skinned mixed-race student. It was as if she did not even have to think about whether or not she would be accepted by faculty and students at whatever college she attended. This could be due to her relative privilege as a lighter-skinned person, not having to think as much as darker folks about where she goes and with whom she associates. Thus, her inattention to the power structures of race has the effect of reinforcing her status, in terms of whose narrative counts ontologically and epistemologically, relative to darker-skinned mixed-race students.

Although Logan did not know that Cliff View College existed until just prior to applying, he, like Samantha, did not choose Cliff View as a means to become more authentically American Indian.

I didn't even know that Cliff View College existed . . . So, as far as me coming here because it's a tribal college . . . it had nothing to do with it. I considered the price a plus, and other than price and being like a federally funded tribal college . . . those things . . . the rest was just gravy. I wish it was closer to home, but that's okay. Still, for the most part . . . I still do not think that the education at this school is on par with state schools. I can say at the same time no other creative writing program in the country can boast the same amount of success as Cliff View College can . . . the same could be said for their new media department. So, it's a real kind of riddle. I don't understand how with the [low] rigor of the courses you have undergraduate students doing such great things after they graduate . . . I mean . . . students getting into Brown and Cornell and . . . NYU.

Stacey had a comparable viewpoint of student expectations at Cliff View College: "Instructors just let some students slide by with whatever. I know several students that did that. It was like that in my geometry class. White teachers here act as if they . . . like they feel bad and they pass you along. It doesn't help you do anything . . . it's sad."

A couple of the students in this category based their decision to attend Cliff View on a need to know more about American Indian culture, but they did not express their reason as a need to prove their Nativeness to "authentic" American Indians. For example, Anthony's decision to attend a tribal college was based on his wanting to have more cultural and historical knowledge. He said, "I am an open-minded individual with a hunger to know more about my personal heritage as well as the heritage of others." And Kim's decision to attend a tribal college was formed out of a wish "just to be in college with other American Indian students." However, her experience at Cliff View soured her experience. After a long hesitation, she stated: "Coming to this college was a big difference for me because people here . . . judge with their eyes and you know . . . they don't actually want to come out and meet you and learn about or just . . . you know?" Kim was still unprepared for the reality of being raced as a mixed-race American Indian at a tribal college. In addition to her slow adjustment to college, "it's just different . . . even if a full-blood Indian I'm talking to . . . it's still different from where I come from. It doesn't matter . . . even what color you are . . . it's just weird. On campus . . . I get made fun of 'cause I'm from Alaska. I think that's really shallow."

Anthony was more direct in his comments about his campus experiences.

On campus there are certain individuals that treat people or act a certain way to appear more Native and more knowledgeable about Native issues.

Although what they do not realize is that we are in school to learn, not prove our Nativeness to each other. And I do believe that instructors show favoritism towards certain students based on their appearance of being Native. Well, being light complexioned, most do not even consider the fact that I am Native and Chicano. So, it always seems that I have to explain myself. And on campus during drum circles, I feel like I don't have a place because I wasn't raised traditionally Native. You know . . . most people have no idea that I am Chicano, Native and gay [laughs]. They just assume I am a white, sixteen-year-old punk. Oh my [laughs]. Well, it seems that on campus they believe the more Native looking you are, the more you know. I'll tell you one thing, I've seen a handful of Natives who are very dark and know nothing about their own cultures. There are certain students and staff members that carry a big chip on their shoulder because they are "more Native." Although there is a big difference between Native Americans who actually practice traditional ways of life and those who play the race card to get away with certain situations without even knowing anything.

Anthony's words bluntly illustrated what some of the students addressed in their conversations about their experiences on campus. At Cliff View, phenotype seems to play a larger role in claims to American Indian authenticity than traditional knowledge. While both are
important to this process, culture is more fluid in that it can be acquired through learning, whereas race, which has the rigid qualities of a caste system, cannot. Whereas lighter-skinned mixed-race students can achieve closer associations with Nativeness despite their whiteness by learning traditional ways, darker-skinned, especially phenotypically black, mixed-race students are kept socially distant regardless of how culturally traditional they become.

Logan commented about his perception of students' experiences on campus identity politics.

We are trying to perpetuate a stereotype here. When it gets to classroom settings and the issue comes up such as . . . blood quantum or skin color, then people do begin to assert their values in a more confident way because they are at a tribal college. So, I think in that academic setting that's where you need to try to establish . . . your views and not just . . . "Well, my parents said this so I need to do that." And so . . . I think in an academic setting . . . you are kinda forced to look down the road . . . as opposed to right now. If you are just looking at blood quantum right now . . . I mean . . . you are just talking about yourself and odds are that you are of the blood quantum that doesn't matter or if you are not the blood quantum . . . whether you are not Indian or whatever . . . you are still here anyways at a tribal college.

Logan thus reiterates a common theme found in this research, namely, that although a tribal college campus such as Cliff View is intended to provide an academic "safe haven" for mixed-race American Indian students, many, especially darker-skinned ones, did not find this to be true. Although Cliff View places an emphasis on culture and tradition, it is still a structure defined by white power dynamics that supports a biological construct of race.

Region seems to also play a factor in the social demarcation of Nativeness. Logan describes how American Indians not from the Southwest were seen as less authentic.

It also has to do with going to college in the Southwest . . . how people characterize you as Native. Back home . . . we joke about the Southwest tribes actually. The joke is that they are the real Indians because they wear turquoise all the time. You know, we come out here for Gathering of Nations and we get the stink eye because we are "civilized" from where we are . . . so, . . . it's just something that you begin to accept and laugh at . . . especially on campus.

Whether students experienced discomfort around, or judgment of, their mixedness, it became clear throughout the interviews and group sessions that their impression of campus life was instrumental in how they viewed the tribal college experience.

Not all of their experiences at Cliff View were negative. Anthony's included "actively participating in Native culture, and it made me want to seek more information about my Native side of my family." Having experienced the pressures of attending a reservation school engulfed in one particular tribal culture, Samantha thought her experience at Cliff View had a positive effect. "I changed my racial identity by feeling more of that race. Like in Window Rock, I felt white, but I would try to feel Native. But here on campus, school makes me feel proud to be Native and it makes me feel more ashamed of being white." However, Samantha seems to contradict herself a bit when she says, "Well, at school since I'm mixed with white . . . and . . . like white is viewed as bad . . . it's hard, so it's kinda encouraged to just say you are

Native." This leaves one to wonder whether she truly feels more American Indian as a result of her experience at Cliff View or if she is simply trying to fit in and avoid conflict.

Logan was more overtly critical of Cliff View. He felt that the focus on authentic Nativeness was often overbearing and essentialist.

> Like in class work . . . in the artwork that they choose to create and even the regalia that they choose as being traditional. So, for example, students during graduation choose to dress up in Native regalia and they choose something that they think is representative of their culture and it might be . . . just to look and feel Indian. And something that looks Indian and for some . . . is wearing buckskins and feathers instead of a traditional ribbon shirt and turbine if you are from the Southeast or whatever.

Logan also candidly states, "People do try to influence . . . my racial identity choice and those people are actually . . . the instructors and administrators here at school."

Through practices that accept the mixedness only of specific groups, the racial and cultural organization of Cliff View College causes Indianness to be narrowly defined. Indianness then becomes based on the social and political environment in which it is being defined and how that particular environment would prefer Indianness to be viewed by others (i.e., not black). Further confounding the topic is that race politics has become institutionalized in higher education at Cliff View College. This institutionalization will redefine current constructs of race, racial identification, and racial classification. It was disheartening to students with black mixedness to see how Cliff View College influenced the role and the defining factors of Indianness. Students faced these situations with peers and faculty in classrooms and in their living environments, whether within their communities or on campus.

The views and situations described by participants indicate the presence of institutionalized racism. The argument put forward by Derrick Bell (1976, 1995) in "Serving Two Masters" is instructive and can be applied to the situation at Cliff View. Bell argued that black children would have been better off without the outcome of the *Brown v. Board of Education* decision. His view is based on the continued widening racial disparities of educational opportunities, with black children remaining disempowered and poor compared to whites. The "two masters" are the deep-seated racial policies of political institutions and the interests being served by a racialized social order. On one hand, tribal colleges began through a seemingly progressive movement of self-determination, but on the other hand they have limited promise because they are "serving two masters." One way the institution, faculty, and certain students are performing such acts is by aligning themselves with race essentialist ideology. And when those who phenotypically fit the stereotype of being American Indian refuse to create an alignment with those who are alienated (phenotypically black or black mixedness), the idea of existing races as pure rather than a social construct for whites to maintain power and privilege is further reinforced.

A second way tribal colleges are "serving two masters" lies in the role these institutions play in competing for funds and resources based on white, oppressive federal and state regulations. For example, the requirements of federal grants do not meet the cultural or traditional missions of tribal colleges, yet predictably, tribal colleges must conform to such Westernized institutional values to access funds. Thus, their missions become governmentally determined instead of self-determined. So it is important to question how education has been used as an oppressive tool to navigate divisive strategies through race identity politics, as described on a more micro level in this study. One of the pressing ethical questions within tribal college learning environments is how to decolonize the Westernized thought process (educational practices, the value of blood quantum, etc.) to focus more on traditional tribal education. Yet, my argument is that even that question is too vague. The more profound question is how do tribal colleges discontinue essentialist practices as more and more tribal communities are becoming mixed race? How will they undo the racial status hierarchies that already structure, thoroughly, American Indian communities? Traditional knowledge alone cannot accomplish this task. For tribal colleges, locating education within the framework of self-determination is critical. However, as Deloria and Wildcat (2001) argue, self-determination is not a self-evident concept. "We must ask ourselves, where is the self-determination? What is it that we as selves and communities are determining? We will find that we are basically agreeing to model our lives, values, and experiences along non-Indian lines" (135). But, as this research has argued, who exactly is non–American Indian? How do these lines get drawn? And what effect does that have on ideas about American Indian community needs? Because tribal colleges need economic support from government agencies, they are not privy to decisions on how policy influences the racial boundaries of political institutions. In fact, as a result of need, most tribal college leaders detach themselves from these racialized boundaries as a means of economic survival, and with this detachment comes assimilation to whiteness. The reality is that as more and more tribal communities become mixed race with blackness, the operations of the culture of white power will continue to function as discriminators against the mixedness of blacks or those deemed blackened.

Mixed-race students' communicated experiences indicate a need to address this population's concern at Cliff View College. In fact, all students at Cliff View would benefit from a curriculum that addressed racial politics within American Indian communities as well as between American Indian and non–American Indian social groups. It is interesting to note that despite their struggles at Cliff View, most of the students did not see a need to change their degree programs nor did they indicate a need to transfer to a different tribal college.

How students' race is asserted, assigned, and reassigned appears to be determined by whether they are mixed with black versus with white or non-black. According to participants, this particular tribal college did not provide a supportive or welcoming environment. As a result, students were highly stratified based on experiences tied to their phenotype and racial mixture.

All students experienced some sort of adjustment to the racial culture of Cliff View College. In the classroom, there was often a divide between mixed-race students with black versus those with white, similar to the differences between monoracial white and black student experiences. As a result of dissimilar experiences based on mixedness, there was group association conflicts during their schooling experiences that included feeling victimized when their whiteness did not prevail as an asset or being alienated due to blackness. Overall, the schooling experiences of mixed race with black indicated situations of racial conflict.

Discussion sessions with the nine students in this study provided a distinctive portrait of the multiracial experience at Cliff View College. Apparent was a profound, clear distinction between the mixed-race black experiences and the mixed-race white experiences based on phenotypic features. The inability of Cliff View College as well as other tribal colleges to break the stigma of "serving two masters" was evident. Race essentialism and strictly defined government funding tightly control the actual project of "self-determination" in tribal colleges. How does this constitute real self-determination? And what does it mean to be "self-determined" if colorism and racial exclusion are the norm in institutions that are supposed to embody progress and empowerment? For Cliff View College, self-determination is structured within a context of social and political culture that is defined by whiteness, which means that "self-determination" is actually positioned to further uphold racial meanings within a racial order.

## Note

1. "Indian Education Act (IEA)—was an amendment to the 815 and 874 impact aid statues of the 1950 Congress. The IEA established the Office of [American] Indian Education. Also, IEA defined 'Indians' very broadly to include communities that did not have formal Interior recognition, and no blood quantum or residency requirements were included which would have limited application of the act" (Deloria 1999, 177).

# PART III
# UNDOING "INDIANNESS"

# 7

# The Notion of "Indianness"

The historic inauguration of our nation's first mixed-race president, Barack Obama, has heightened the need to discuss the issues that surround the meaning of race. For many reasons, President Obama's mixed-race background embodies the social and political gaps perpetuated by skin color and the material value of one's mixedness. As President Obama states:

> I am the son of a black man from Kenya and white woman from Kansas. I was raised with the help of a white grandfather, who survived a depression to serve in Patton's Army during World War II, and a white grandmother, who worked on a bomber assembly line at Fort Leavenworth while he was over-seas. I've gone to some of the best schools in America and lived in one of the world's poorest nations. I am married to a black American who carries within her the blood of slaves and slave owners—an inheritance we pass on to our two precious daughters. (Obama 2008)

President Obama's mixedness cannot be understood or assessed without a logical frame of reference. In multiple respects, identity choice among

DOI: 10.5876/9781607325444.c007

mixed-race people who may have idealized attaining whiteness will only perpetuate the manifestations of race and its pervasiveness in upholding a racialized dichotomy. Thus, I see on one hand those who are stained by the essentialist notions of skin color being continually denigrated, while on the other hand I see those of a certain mixedness and phenotypic features being complicitous in colorism. On one side, there is the common problem of (not) belonging due to how we learn to see race and sort people accordingly. On the other side, there is the less studied problem of how mixed-race people internalize the value of whiteness and perpetuate the very system that creates their alienation in the first place.

## Recognizing and Confronting Racial Realities

This research sought to determine how multiracial students conform to and/ or resist racial privilege and to what extent their experiences within political institutions influence their racial identity choice. Critical Race Theory helped me to unveil the theoretical, conceptual, and pedagogical experiences related to mixed-race experiences at Cliff View College. In multiple respects, using a qualitative inquiry approach seen through the lens of Critical Race Theory to analyze the discourse and lived experiences of mixed-race participants challenged how a tribal college operated in troubling ways by oppressing, marginalizing, and denigrating mixed-race with black students but not mixed-race with white students, who benefited from their whiteness and found ways to navigate the institution. Through the use of discourse as a component of CRT analysis, I have practiced Ladson-Billings's (1999) perspective: "The voice of people of color is required for a deep understanding of the educational system" (16). And as the discourse is structured around the lived experience of those of a certain mixedness, then that structure provides a framework prearranged by the meaning of race.

Soloranzo and Yosso (2002) further assert that, "A critical race theory challenges the traditional claims that educational institutions make toward objectivity, meritocracy, colorblindness, race neutrality, and equal opportunity" (26). And this study's methodology challenged the traditional paradigms and theories that often portray all mixed-race people as victims, while exposing the historical context of race and the multiple layers of oppression and discrimination within a tribal college that places emphasis on cultural and traditional art forms as a means of self-determination. As Soloranzo and Yosso explain, "If methodologies have been used to silence and marginalize people of color, then methodologies can also give voice and turn the margins into places of transformative resistance" (37). For many reasons, Critical Race Theory was used as a tool to explain the sustained inequalities of a racial hierarchy and the connections to mixed-race identity choice.

The definition and supportive arguments of CRT scholars (Allen 2006; Bonilla-Silva and Embrick 2006; Crenshaw et al. 1995; Delagado and Stefancic 2001; Foster 2005; Leonardo 2005; Soloranzo and Yosso 2002) provide a lens of insight to identify and analyze how the cultural structure of political institutions maintains a racialized social order. Although race and racism are the focal points of a critical race analysis, such investigation also divulges the layers of multiraciality and how certain mixedness can then be viewed as a symbolic form of material value—that is, that lighter carries more value than darker. As explained by Lewis (2003), "Race, and specifically within our current context, whiteness, can then be considered as a form of symbolic capital—a resource that may be accessed or deployed to provide access to additional resources" (171). And as a result of the culture of political institutions having influencing factors in both informal and formal lived experiences, there are multiple forms of white privilege and power at play.

The findings at Cliff View College, simply stated, were that the experiences of mixed-race with black versus mixed-race with white students did not support the political stances commonly associated with academic discourses on multiraciality (victimization, fluid racial identity, eliminating race, etc.). Although most participants reported at least some feelings of alienation from the American Indian community, it is also true that their views about being mixed-race people varied depending on where they were racially positioned. These differences were also related to varying awareness about the experiences of mixed-race people and the operation of race more generally. This suggests that rather than challenging race as we know it, mixed-race people are in fact racialized and positioned; they are not, in actuality, without a race because, more important, they have a racial *position* in the racial status order of Cliff View and the larger society.

In this study, the educational institution played a role in the racialization of mixed-race students. Cliff View, as a tribal college with a strong history of focusing on self-determination, did not institutionally act in ways that are

compatible with the meaning of self-determination, nor did it appear to critique its institutional day-to-day practices of oppression. Despite its own history of being oppressed as an institution that serves American Indian people,
it eroded the credibility of its supposed political stance against the historically racist attitudes of "educating the Indian" as well as more hidden aspects
of inequality. After all, European colonization and the construction of race
are two sides of the same coin. One cannot claim to be decolonized until
racial practices have been ended. It is clear that Cliff View has a long way to
go to decolonize its racial practices. By continually upholding white supremacist notions to devise opportunities to instill internalized racism, Cliff View
College is institutionally assimilating the meaning of whiteness and bestow-
ing more privilege on those who serve the larger political interests of whites
(Allen 2004; Bell 1995; Tatum 1997). Self-determination and the elimination of
racism, including colorism and featurism, must be co-extensive. Submission
to the value of lighter skin is in no way a form of self-determination.

The findings of this study revealed that lived experiences, in particular
experiences at Cliff View College, were influenced by certain mixedness.
Mixed race with black and mixed race with white were the basic perspectives
for the emergence of three major themes: (1) racial(ized) self-perceptions, (2)
peer interaction and influences, and (3) impact on academic experiences. The
nine mixed-raced participants' perceptions of the material value of race in
their formal and informal schooling experiences contributed to the context
of the discourse they used to describe their mixedness, and even influenced
their own mixed-race identity choices. Connolly and Troyna (1998) explains
how race operates as a material value within institutions:

> It is clearly the case that white skin, for instance, can represent symbolic capi-
> tal in certain contexts. Some teachers may be influenced (whether directly or
> indirectly) by a set of racist beliefs which encourages them to think of white
> children as being more intelligent and well behaved than black children. In this
> sense, having white skin represents a form of symbolic capital which brings
> with it better treatment and more educational opportunities. (21)

Further, Lewis (2003) argue that "race can be thought of as a symbolic
or signifying system that serves as an instrument of communication and
knowledge (tells us things about people before we even know them) and as
an instrument of domination that sorts and ranks groups" (171). Race as a

symbolic factor could be seen in participants' perceptions. Those who were mixed race with white and phenotypically light complexioned viewed their lived experiences as "a great opportunity," "an advantage." These students said things like: "Because I look white, I'm often judged different from the rest of my friends who look Native or Hispanic"; "People just see me as white . . . I'm not always treated different"; "In class, they just assume that I'm smarter because of the way I look"; and "I look white . . . so . . . it's just different for me."

Ladson-Billings (1999) eloquently explained the importance of "voices" to understand the racist inequalities of education structured within institutions. A different lens comes out of the experiences of those who are black/ American Indian mixed-race people. The "voices" of these participants affirm that their identity options are anything but fluid advantages. These affirmations are captured in statements like the following: "Phenotypically it is like, obviously, they say she's just a black girl. Here at this school [Cliff View College] . . . I wonder if it would have been seen easier for me to say, 'I'm black'"; "You can't be Native . . . you are part black"; and "I find that a lot of people here [Cliff View College] carry a lot of racial and prejudice baggage. All I can say is that there is a major difference between having white blood in you." The "voices" of those who are mixed race with black and phenotypically darker complexioned allude to hidden racial agendas that demarcate racial boundaries and influence the meanings of mixed-race identities. Identity is not simply a choice for those who are alienated and denigrated. Others who aspire to attain whiteness assign it to them and draw distinctions.

Although the majority of educators at Cliff View College identify as American Indian, it is also true that they are mostly people who are mixed race with white. Their perceptions of race provided the context and setting that reinforced stereotypes and racialized experiences, thus influencing the mixed-race identity choices of students. Other mixed-race with black students had similar stories: "I'm viewed as black even though I identify with my Native American heritage more often"; and "But it seems like . . . especially here at school [Cliff View College] . . . it's like . . . oh . . . well . . . you are pretending or you couldn't possibly be." The phrases "more Native," "viewed as black," and "you couldn't possibly be" indicate that at Cliff View College there are no racial options for mixed-race with black students other than "black." In this way, identity choice is institutionally and socially structured.

Findings further indicated that those who identified as mixed race with white who witnessed acts of alienation or denigration by educators and peers remained silent and did not challenge such behavior, thus performing race through their multiraciality. For example, a mixed-race with white participant stated, "Living in Farmington, New Mexico . . . It was just difficult for me than other Natives. No one was really mean to me because they peg me as white or look at me as white. Other Natives had problems but not me . . . so . . . it's kind of an advantage."

And while mixed race with white has been understood by participants to have a specific, symbolic material value, a similar example of acknowledging racial inequalities by performing race and remaining silent, not challenging racist behavior, was revealed in the following statement: "A lot of people just think I'm white, but they sure don't think I'm Mexican [laughs] and definitely not Native. My friends sometime catch a lot of crap from other people because they are dark. That never happens to me. I wouldn't want to have to deal with that . . . I never have to deal with that."

## De-racing Schools as Race Makes Spaces

Institutional racism and white privilege have become embedded in the deeper, subtle layers in the meaning behind identity choices of multiracial students. Therefore, when trying to understand the persistence of racism and whiteness as forms of high symbolic and material value, it is not enough just to examine the realm of individual choice and the influences of a marginalized institution, such as Cliff View College. One must look at the structural context that manifests symbolic material value into reproducing racism from a macro lens (Omi and Winant 1994). In this study, the larger structures of racism manifested through the discourse around defining one's Indianness. There is a contradiction in that on one hand whiteness exoticizes Indianness, but on the other hand, as seen from a "macro" perspective, whites need allies, including even those who become defined as "Native," to maintain power. As one mixed-race participant explained, "More and more tribes are going white; it's the popular trend." This statement is an example of the influences of a racialized social system within the United States. This assimilation of white privilege is often invisible and unacknowledged by tribes. Tribes participating as the oppressors are clouded, and they show little willingness to be empathetic toward the symbolic, material value of the layers of brown-ness and, in particular, blackness in their midst. Instead, these acts of inter-nalized racist ideology fragment and divide raced groups while also creating rank-ordered, caste-like structures. Those with a specific mixedness have a group inroad to Indianness, unlike others, which only serves the larger polit-ical interests of whites in that it reifies the condition where whiter and more European-looking and European-sounding bodies are assigned higher value (Allen 2004; Bell 1995; Tatum 1997).

The situation becomes further compounded when multiraciality is viewed as the answer to debunking race. From a macro lens, a mixed-race reality is neither fluid nor does it simply by existing improve race relations. At Cliff View College, the perspective of mixed-race participants most often upheld the notion of "laissez-faire racism" (Bobo and Smith 1998). When comparing mixed-race with black participants to the meaning of Indianness through a white lens of influence, Bobo and Smith pinpoint that "laissez-faire racism is based on cultural inferiority" (186). And with cultural superiority having an economic and political value, the opposite, cultural inferiority, is then based on "a historical analysis of the changing economics and politics of race in the United States" (187). Race has been defined and positioned as an economic and political tool within a racial hierarchy. And a mixed-race with white person enrolled as a member in a state or federally recognized tribe has both an economic and political value that influences the definition of one's Indianness. The concept of laissez-faire racism is applied not only to people who are raced as monoracially black, but also people who are mixed race with black with specific phenotypic features. This provides a more adequate lens for viewing the influencing factors of a certain mixedness conforming to a racialized social system and why one's Indianness as mixed race with black is culturally inferior to mixed race with white.

I hoped to develop a deeper understanding about the mixed-race experience within a tribal college setting. I wanted to help articulate and understand the lived experiences of mixed-race students within a white supremacist context. More specifically, I sought to contextualize students' representation of their racial identity choices through the compounded race politics of blood quan-tum and stereotypes of phenotypic features. The purpose of such inquiry was to shed light on the misconceptions of being mixed race (fluid identity, eliminating race, resisting a racialized social system, etc.) and, in turn, on how Indianness has been interpreted as a major factor in determining membership within these types of peer groups. My intent was to provide insight to describe and explain more fully the formal and informal lived experiences of mixed-raced with black and mixed-race with white American Indian students. This explanation, that colorism plays a majoring role in shaping students' feelings of belonging, could in turn assist educational organizations in evaluating their own institutional and educational practices in regard to race.

As I gathered data and analyzed its contents in an ongoing manner consistent with ground theory methodology, I realized that overall the mixed-race students' experiences were heavily influenced by an institution that aligns with societal norms, regardless of its status as a tribal college. I found that there were different experiences unique to mixed-race with white and mixed-race with black students. While both category of students experienced the effect of feeling on the other side of American Indian boundary demarcations, the experience of mixed-race with blacks students was much more denigrating and exclusionary. In fact, there were many ways in which mixed-race with white students were privileged relative to other students, including those students who were not seen as mixed race. Not only were the specific needs of students not articulated, they also went unrecognized by the institution. Although participants, especially mixed race with white students, described numerous ways they conformed to the practice of racial hierarchy and colorism at Cliff View, there were occasions when resistance was mentioned. However, these forms of resistance seemed to do little to prevent their being assigned a racial status in ways consistent with the larger racial structure of the United States.

The theory resulting from this study identifies family, peers, and institutions as major influencing factors in defining a mixed-race student's experience at a tribal college. The family has a strong role in influencing the symbolic, material value of race and a student's interactions with racial issues, even at the collegiate level. Race impacts much of the student experience in a university environment, from introduction to the campus to roommates to peers. Currently there is very little research that examines how race is asserted, assigned, and negotiated as a mixed-race experience at a tribal college. This study illustrates that there is indeed a direct racialized impact, and that this impact also has implications for the definition and practice of "cultural heritage" and "Nativeness."

Peer interactions also influenced the mixed-race student's experience at Cliff View College. Acceptance or rejection by peers contributes to students' sense of racial identity and often magnifies the psychological effect of their mixed-race background. Students are reminded, both subtly and overtly, in and outside of the classroom, that they do not fit neatly and completely into a monoracial American Indian category. The impact is even stronger for some students who, because of their black phenotypic appearance, are not acknowledged as American Indian within the campus and community culture of Cliff View College. Examining peer interactions outside of the classroom is not a new phenomenon of research on students' experiences within a college environment. However, the mixed-race student experience, in particular the experience of mixed-race American Indian students in a tribal college setting, differs slightly from what current research offers, especially since it has been conducted at mostly majority white schools. By focusing on a tribal college whose students are mostly students of color, we can see how the privileging of whiteness functions hegemonically among people of color, even in a space that is allegedly "theirs." Within the highly racialized confines of Cliff View College, these students' experiences are continually influencing their notions of who they are, and the social actors in the institution draw lines defining who they are not.

Overall, I believe that my research findings broaden and deepen the understanding of the tribal college experience and its impact on mixed-race American Indian identity choice experience. The findings demonstrate further the reinforcement of race as a social construct, in particular the role phenotypic appearance plays in one's connection to a tribal college community. Moreover, each student's experience in this study was shown to impact identity disposition in more powerful ways. It's this disposition regarding identity choice politics that re-fabricates races as a material value.

# 8

# Reenvisioning Tribal Colleges through CRT and Tribal Critical Race Theory

This study's results provide tribal colleges and other institutes of higher education with important issues to consider as they seek to provide a learning environment for an increasing population of mixed-race American Indian students. The students' stories shed light on frustrations that need to be addressed. Although tribal colleges have not yet done so, they can deal with these frustrations and take a proactive approach in preparing for the experiences of mixed-race students. Furthermore, since the experiences of mixed-race students are influenced by colorism and racial hierarchy, processes that all students are involved in and affected by, critical proactive approaches could have positive effects for the entire student body. Institutions, in particular tribal colleges, will want to evaluate how to address the situation of the mixed-race population immediately as well as in the long term. The self-determination premise pressures tribal colleges to retain students, so thus tribal colleges should encourage inquiry into lived experiences on campus and the teaching of anti-racist curricula, including a critical focus on the racialization of the growing populations of mixed-raced students in American Indian communities.

DOI: 10.5876/9781607325444.c008

Theoretically, this work demonstrates that it is important to study not only what people *say* about mixed-race American Indian identities and racial issues, but also what they *do* in a particular context. Through a CRT lens, race is seen as a social construction, but it is also understood to have very real effects—cultural, psychological, and material. For this reason, a number of recommendations can be drawn from CRT, but it is also important to include Tribal Critical Race Theory (TribalCrit) to acknowledge an endemic process of neo-colonial forms of colonization that have become ingrained interactional practices within education systems relevant to Indigenous peoples (Brayboy 2005). The theories are complementary. CRT views race and racism as endemic to society, while TribalCrit emphasizes that colonization is endemic to society (Brayboy 2005). I agree with Alfred (2004) that "the university is contentious ground" (192). It is important to understand the racial formation process in a tribal college setting, including daily racialization and renegotiation of racial boundaries by serving an important role as "Indigenous academics." As Alfred (2004) states, "We need to turn away from defining our purpose and methods by Western academic standards and be accountable to our cultural heritage and to our people" (95). This recommendation address ways to enhance the college experiences, both in and out of class, that contribute to students' sense of identity, which also translates into enhancing the awareness of identity politics influenced by blood quantum and a racialized social system that upholds whiteness as having a material value.

More important, these strategies should be shared with higher educational professionals, particularly those whose primary responsibility is to prepare students with the skills to succeed in a learning environment while promoting a critical perspective of the daily effects of systemic racism and colonization (Alfred 2004; Brayboy 2005; Justice 2004; Mihesuah 2004). Unfortunately, most often, instructors and staff who assist students academically, socially, and culturally at Cliff View College tend to utilize the traditional paradigm of being raced based on one's essentialized degree of Indianness. A solution would be to "Indigenize the academy." According to Alfred (2004), "it means that we are working to change universities so that they become places where the values, principles, and modes of organization and behavior of our people are respected in, and hopefully even integrated into, the larger system of structures and processes that make up the university itself" (88). Educating key staff who work directly with mixed-race students who identify as American Indian or acknowledge their American Indian heritage about educational equality is the first step. Then, just as critical and more challenging, step two is educating the larger body of Cliff View College instructors, staff, and administrators about how educational environments are used as audiences to re-fabricate a race-based ideology. One example is how instructors on campus lower their expectations for American Indian students or play into stereotypes of government-funded programs for such students. Even worse, some instructors assume that students attending a tribal college want to learn how to be "Indian." As Brayboy (2005) asserts, "The colonization has been so complete that even many American Indians fail to recognize that we are taking up colonialist ideas when we fail to express ourselves in ways that may challenge dominant society's ideas about who and what we are supposed to be, how we are supposed to behave, and what we are supposed to be within the larger population" (431). Certainly staff, instructors, and administrators need knowledge of how to challenge colonization tactics to appropriately strategize how to avoid reproducing oppressive learning environments. Brayboy writes, "Knowledge is defined by TribalCrit as the ability to recognize change, adapt, and move forward with the change" (434). However, I would contend that most higher education professionals do not recognize the need for critical learning about racial, not just cultural, issues and how such discourse can improve the educational experience. Instructors, staff, and administrators need to have a grasp of traditional cultural paradigms to understand the experience of a certain mixedness being denigrated or alienated. What they must have at Cliff View College is the sense of responsibility to combat racial privilege and assist students with academic success, while providing a healthy, supportive learning environment.

Finally, upon reading this study and similar works of research, administrations at institutions of higher education have the opportunity to replace models and practices that work to support the social and political structures of white privilege. They can create policies and practices that acknowledge the current social complexities in which students exist, and choose to support and validate students' experiences as they progress in their academic endeavors. Yet, they also need to be courageous enough to challenge student views that support colorism and structural racism. Cliff View College must evaluate how it can best assist mixed-race students in critically understanding their racial positionality, its structural origins, and its relative privilege and/

or disprivilege. And since non-mixed-raced students are also involved in this process, they need to be engaged in a critical curriculum that situates them as active, resistant agents who confront past and present practices that perpetuate colorism and an essentialized "Nativeness."

## Reenvisioning Self-Determination

Administrators should provide programs for students to help them prepare for the developmental milestones they will confront during their college years. Administrators also need to make connections to mixed-race American Indian students to ensure that the cultural climate of the college is supportive of student success. Administrators should provide positive opportunities for students to immerse themselves in their own culture as well as interact with and learn cultures outside their own. Administrators should ensure that professional development sensitizes faculty and staff to the culture of the community and the growing body of mixed-race students who identify as American Indian. In addition, administrators should provide support systems for students. Programs should include family support to the greatest degree possible so that students' families support their self-determination. One of the best ways administrators can help is to seek out faculty who bring a critical race perspective to their pedagogy and scholarship.

For faculty and staff, focusing on the individual through the use of empowering strategies, and being in tune with their own racial ideologies will help students develop positive connections and views of all raced groups. By being aware of, and critically reflecting on, their own racial ideologies, faculty and staff can transform their thinking about the issues or race, colorism, and colonialism as they play out in American Indian communities and schools (Alfred 2004; Brayboy 2005; Justin 2004; Mihesuah 2004). They need to be aware of how students experience racialized politics of American Indian identity and blood quantum politics within a tribal college environment. As Mihesuah (2004) states, "One of the most pressing issues for a Native student is identity. Many Natives, even those who are full blood, often have intense identity issues" (194). Faculty and staff should, both in words and actions, believe in all possibilities for students and have high expectations of students regardless of their phenotypic appearance, and they should be clued in to how phenotype creates a more negative environment for those who are darker skinned.

"Cultural competence," popular among multiculturalists, and structural racial knowledge need to be integrated into the whole curriculum, but specific classes also need to be offered to address Indianness, racial identity politics, and the influence of blood quantum. Mihesuah (2004) presents this position on a personalized sense of oppression: "Internalized colonization (called the 'boarding school syndrome' among many Native Activists), is the phenomenon of believing that whites and their culture are superior, accepting negative stereotypes about Natives, not questioning biased classroom lectures, and acting negatively toward other Natives" (194). In other words, these problems should be made a major part of the overt curriculum, not repressed and swept under the rug in the hope that they will just go away on their own. Faculty should welcome a critical approach to racism and racial knowledge in the classroom for all students as opposed to viewing specific components as relevant to only a specific raced group. They should help students better understand the connections between blood quantum and its effects on self-determination for American Indians, positive and negative. But more important, students should have a better understanding of the pedagogical strategies used as oppressive tools in learning environments so that they can better resist their damaging effects.

There are multiple areas for future study that could include both qualitative and quantitative methods analyzed through both CRT and TribalCrit lenses. Since there are currently thirty-six tribal colleges, many of the issues at Cliff View College are parallel to issues among other mixed-race students in cultural and traditional environments.

While the establishment of a mixed-race student services office may not be deemed necessary by the mixed-race students in this study, they articulated that their experiences are different from those who monoracially identify as American Indian. Moreover, the experiences of mixed-race persons of white versus black heritage are especially dissimilar, which is a profound reason to further explore the meaning of whiteness and blackness within American Indian populations and institutions. Also worth analyzing is discourse used by mixed-race students at tribal colleges that border black communities compared to those that border white communities. Two students in this study, with vastly different appearances, felt the same lack of connection to the campus community because of their experiences with colorism, not being enrolled tribal members, the notion of race being based on (allegedly) cultural characteristics at Cliff View College (cultural values, norms, social standing), and phenotypic appearance.

As more and more mixed-race students enroll at tribal colleges, it illuminates the need to confront colonized and racialized realities. As Justice (2004) explains, "If Nationhood and liberation are our goals, we must truly acknowledge the diversity of Native experiences by avoiding both the traps of 'mixed-blood angst' and of 'full-blood purity'—if we focus on blood quantum as an indicator of Indian authenticity, we emphasize a colonialist paradigm" (104). However, as I have tried to emphasize throughout this book, if we take seriously the fact that race is a social construction, we must pay attention to how racialized processes work: continuing discrimination and institutional racism, perpetuating and exacerbating old forms of colonialism, and reinforcing neocolonialism. If tribal colleges and other institutions continue to reproduce learning environments where students perform race and act racially, they will need to delve deeply into the impact on those students. Additionally, tribal colleges and other institutions should be interested in learning more about the impact of schooling influences on mixed-race identity choice when classroom, campus, and peer pressures assert and assign certain mixedness to a particular group. If for no other reason, tribal colleges, as a new form of self-determination in comparison to historically black colleges and universities, will want to attract, retain, and graduate this growing population of students. Beyond academics, one of the main reasons students do not complete their education at tribal colleges and other institutions is the lack of social and cultural connections on campus, among their peers, and within the learning environment. Tribal colleges and other institutions will want to develop programs and services to help these students identify and bond with their learning environments.

One of my goals in conducting this study was to provide mixed-race American Indian students attending tribal colleges with the opportunity to read about the experiences of others so they can see that they are not alone. It was interesting and enjoyable to interview the students and hear their stories. They have unique experiences that should be widely shared. My hope is that this study will contribute to the understanding of the factors that shape mixed-race identity within politicized institutions, such as schools, and highlight the importance of educating to empower.

# Appendix A

## First Participant Interview

*Questions on Identity*

PARENTS / FAMILY / HOME:

1. Explain how the topic of race is discussed in your family.
2. How are you shaping your identity or choosing how to racially identify yourself? In what specific ways? Does anyone try to influence your racial identity choice? Who?
3. Who or what was the biggest contributor(s) to your racial identity?
4. What racial identity choice do your parents encourage?
5. Do you feel accepted by your extended family? Explain.

PEERS / FRIENDSHIP / DATING:

1. How would you describe the racial identities of your friendship groups?
2. Do you have friends who are mixed? Describe how (if) you talk about being mixed race with each other.

DOI: 10.5876/9781607325444.c009

3. What is the racial identity of your significant other?

4. Describe your experiences with dating.

SCHOOL:

1. Describe the first time you recall realizing in school that you are racially different from others.

    Probe(s):

    1a. How do people react to you in terms of racial identity? What do they assume about your racial identity? What sorts of things do they say?

2. What messages do or did you receive about your race from school? Teachers? Principal? Other staff? Peers?

3. Tell me a story that captures what it means to be mixed race to you.

    Probe(s):

    3a. Share with me an example of a time at school when you felt you received a positive message about multiraciality.

    3b. Share with me an example of a time at school when you felt you received a negative message about multiracialty.

# Appendix B

DOI: 10.5876/9781607325444.c010

## Second Participant Interview

*Questions on Identity*

REFLECTIONS ON RACE:

1. What types of names, either positive or negative, can you remember people (of all races) calling you? What sorts of things do they say?
2. In your experiences, in what way has school influenced your racial identity choice(s)? Will you share some of these with me now?
3. Who or what has been the biggest contributor(s) to your racial identity?
4. Explain any changes you've experienced in how you understand your racial identity.
5. Do you think you act differently around people depending on their race? Why? When?
6. Do you feel being mixed race is an advantage, a disadvantage, or neither? Explain.

7. Tell me about a time at school in which you were aware of your mixed-race identity.

   Probe(s):

   7a. Can you tell me a time when you were with someone (perhaps a friend, classmate, or teacher) and you told this person about your racial background? What did you say?

   7b. Please give me an example of how you have expressed your mixed-race identity.

8. Tell me about a time in school in which you changed your racial identity choice to feel accepted or comfortable among peers or teachers.

   Probe(s):

   8a. What does "passing" mean for you? For mixed-race students?

   8b. Can you tell me a time when you changed your racial identity choice to avoid being labeled as a unintelligent, unattractive, or a troublemaker in school?

   8c. Does skin color play a significant role in switching your racial identity?

   8d. Have you ever tried to change your physical appearance (e.g., going to a tanning salon, using skin lighteners, trying different hair products)? For what purposes?

9. Describe the racial climate at your school.

   Probe(s):

   9a. In your school experiences, have there been times when you where very conscious of your race? Will you share some of these with me now?

   9b. Can you tell me a time when you knew someone was being racist against another person because of their racial identity?

   9c. Please give me an example of how students, teachers, the principal, or other staff may have contributed to racism.

10. Is there anything that your school provides that you feel strengthens your racial identity? Is there anything else you wish was provided that was not?

    Probe(s):

    10a. Do you feel that your classroom resources reflect a positive image of being mixed race?

# Appendix C

## Participant Characteristics

|          | Class level | Mother | Father | Identifies as |
|----------|-------------|--------|--------|---------------|
| TONY     | Freshman    | Creole/black | American Indian/black | Black/mixed Race |
| STACEY   | Sophomore   | American Indian | Hispanic/white | American Indian |
| ANTHONY  | Freshman    | Hispanic/American Indian/white | Hispanic | Hispanic |
| SAMANTHA | Freshman    | American Indian/white | American Indian | American Indian/white |
| KATHY    | Senior      | American Indian/black/white | American Indian/black/white | American Indian/mixed race |
| LOGAN    | Freshman    | American Indian/white | American Indian | American Indian |
| KIM      | Freshman    | American Indian/white | American Indian | American Indian |
| JENNIFER | Junior      | Taino (Indigenous)/Hispanic | Taino (Native) | Taino (Indigenous)/Hispanic |
| AMY      | Sophomore   | American Indian/Hispanic/white | White | Mixed race |

DOI: 10.5876/9781607325444.c011

# References

Alfred, T. 2004. "Warrior Scholarship." In *Indigenizing the Academy: Transforming and Empowering Communities*, ed. A. Mihesuah and A. C. Wilson, 88–99. Lincoln: University of Nebraska Press.

Allen, R. 2004. "Whiteness and Critical Pedagogy." *Educational Philosophy and Theory* 36 (2): 121–36. http://dx.doi.org/10.1111/j.1469-5812.2004.00056.x.

Allen, R. 2005. "Whiteness and Critical Pedagogy." In *Critical Pedagogy and Race*, ed. Z. Leonardo, 53–68. Malden, MA: Blackwell.

Allen, R. 2006. "The Race Problem in the Critical Pedagogy Community." In *Reinventing Critical Pedagogy*, ed. R. L. Allen, M. Pruyn, and R. L. Allen, 3–20. Lanham, MD: Rowman & Littlefield.

Anzaldua, G. 1999. "Nos/ostros: 'Us' vs. 'Them,' (des) Conocimientos y Compromisos." Presented at the conference Territories and Boundaries: Geographies of Latindad, University of Illinois, Urbana, October.

Baker, R. W., and B. Siryk. 1984. "Measuring Adjustment to College." *Journal of Counseling Psychology* 31 (2): 179–89. http://dx.doi.org/10.1037/0022-0167.31.2.179.

Bell, D. 1976. "Serving Two Masters: Integration Ideals and Client Interests in School Desegregation Litigation." *The Yale Law Journal* 85 (4): 470–56.

Bell, D. 1995. "Serving Two Masters: Integration Ideals and Client Interests in School Desegregation Litigation." In *Critical Race Theory: The Key Writings That*

DOI: 10.5876/9781607325444.c012

*Formed the Movement*, ed. K. Crenshaw, N. Gotwanda, G. Peller, and K. Thomas, 95–99. New York: New York University Press.

Bettez, S. C. 2007. "Secret Agent Insiders to Whiteness: Mixed Race Women Negotiating Structure and Agency." PhD diss., University of North Carolina at Chapel Hill.

Blumer, H. 1958. "Race Prejudice as a Sense of Group Position." *Pacific Sociological Review* 1 (1): 3–7. http://dx.doi.org/10.2307/1388607.

Bobo, L., and R. Smith. 1998. "From Jim Crow Racism to Laissez-faire Racism." In *Beyond Pluralism: The Conception of Groups and Group Identities in America*, ed. W. Katkin, N. Landsman, and A. Tyree, 182–220. Urbana: University of Illinois Press.

Bogden, R., and S. Biklen. 1998. *Qualitative Research in Education: An Introduction to Theory and Methods*. Boston: Allyn & Bacon.

Bonilla-Silva, E. 1996. "Rethinking Racism: Toward a Structural Interpretation." *American Sociological Review* 62 (June): 465–80.

Bonilla-Silva, E. 2001. *White Supremacy and Racism in the Post–Civil Rights Era*. Boulder, CO: Lynne Rienner.

Bonilla-Silva, E. 2003. *Racism without Racists: Color-blind Racism and the Persistence of Racial Inequality in the United States*. Lanham, MD: Rowman & Littlefield.

Bonilla-Silva, E. 2005. "Racism and New Racism: The Contours of Racial Dynamics in Contemporary America." In *Critical Pedagogy and Race*, ed. Z. Leonardo, 51–68. Malden, MA: Blackwell.

Bonilla-Silva, E., and D. Embrick. 2006. "Black, Honorary White, White: The Future of Race in the United States?" In *Mixed Messages: Multiracial Identities in the "Color-blind" Era*, ed. D. L. Brusma, 33–48. Boulder, CO: Lynne Rienner.

Bourdieu, P. 1986. "The Forms of Capital." In *Handbook of Theory and Research for the Sociology of Education*, ed. J. G. Richardson, 241–58. Westport, CT: Greenwood.

Brayboy, B. M. J. 2005. "Toward a Tribal Critical Race Theory in Education." *Urban Review* 37 (5): 425–46. http://dx.doi.org/10.1007/s11256-005-0018-y.

Byrd, A. D., and L. L. Tharps. 2001. *Hair Story: Untangling Roots of Black Hair in America*. New York: St. Martin's Griffin.

Calleroz, M. D. 2003. "The Experience of Mixed Race Students in Higher Education." PhD diss., Arizona State University.

Chandler, D. L. 1997. "In Shift, Many Anthropologists See Race as Social Construct." *Boston Globe*, May 11, A30.

Connolly, P., and B. Troyna. 1998. *Researching Racism in Education: Politics, Theory, and Practice*. Buckingham, UK: Open University Press.

Corrin, W. J. 2009. "Does Whiteness Matter? Comparing the School Experiences of Mixed-Race Students in Grades Seven through Eleven." PhD diss., Northwestern University.

Cramer, R. A. 2005. *Cash, Color, and Colonialism: The Politics of Tribal Acknowledgement*. Norman: University of Oklahoma Press.

Crenshaw, K., N. Gotanda, G. Peller, and K. Thomas, eds. 1995. *Critical Race Theory: The Key Writings That Formed the Movement*. New York: New Press.

Creswell, J. W. 1998. *Qualitative Inquiry and Research Design: Choosing among Five Traditions*. Thousand Oaks, CA: Sage.

Cruz, B. 2001. *Multiethnic Teens and Cultural Identity*. Berkeley Heights, NJ: Enslow.

Cummins, J. 1996. *Negotiating Identities: Education for Empowerment in a Diverse Society*. Los Angeles: California Association for Bilingual Education.

DaCosta, K. M. 2007. *Making Multiracials: State, Family, and Market in the Redrawing of the Colorline*. Stanford, CA: Stanford University Press.

Dalmage, H. M. 2003. *Tripping the Color Line: Black-White Multiracial Families in a Racially Divided World*. New Brunswick, NJ: Rutgers University Press.

Delagado, R., and J. Stefancic. 2001. *Critical Race Theory: An Introduction*. New York: New York University Press.

Deloria, P. J. 1998. *Playing Indian*. New Haven, CT: Yale University Press.

Deloria, V., Jr. 1999. *Spirit and Reason: The Vine Deloria Reader*. Golden, CO: Fulcrum.

Deloria, V., Jr., and D. Wildcat. 2001. *Power and Place: Indian Education in America*. Golden, CO: Fulcrum.

Delpit, L. 1995. *Other People's Children: Cultural Conflict in the Classroom*. New York: New Press.

Denzin, N., and Y. Lincoln, eds. 2000. *The Handbook of Qualitative Research*. Thousand Oaks, CA: Sage.

Fernandez, C. 1995. "Testimony of the Association of Multiethnic Americans before the Subcommittee on Census, Statistics and Postal Personnel of the U.S. House of Representatives." In *American Mixed Race: The Culture of Microdiversity*, ed. N. Zack, 191–210. Lanham, MD: Rowman & Littlefield.

Foster, M. 2005. "Race, Class, and Gender in Education Research: Surveying the Political Terrain." In *Critical Pedagogy and Race*, ed. Z. Leonardo, 175–83. Malden, MA: Blackwell.

Gallagher, C. A. 2004. "Racial Redistricting: Expanding the Boundaries of Whiteness." In *The Politics of Multiracialism: Challenging Racial Thinking*, ed. H. M. Dalmage, 59–76. Albany: State University of New York Press.

Garroutte, E. M. 2003. *Real Indians: Identity and the Survival of Native America*. Berkley: University of California Press.

Goldberg, D. T. 2001. "States of Whiteness." In *Between Law and Culture: Relocating Legal Studies*, ed. D. T. Goldberg, M. Musheno, and L. Bower, 174–94. Minneapolis: University of Minnesota Press.

Hall, R. 2008. "Manifestations of Racism in the 21st Century." In *Racism in the 21st Century: An Empirical Analysis of Skin Color*, ed. H. Hall, 25–44. New York: Springer Science & Business Media, LLC. http://dx.doi.org/10.1007/978-0-387-79098-5_2.

hooks, b. 1992. "Revolutionary Renegades: Native Americans, African Americans and Black Indians." In *Black Looks: Race and Representation*, 179–94. Boston: South End.

Hunter, M. L. 2005. *Race, Gender, and the Politics of Skin Tone*. New York: Routledge.

Jones, L. 1995. "Is Biracial Enough? Or, What's This about a Multiracial Category on the Census? A Conversation." In *Bulletproof Diva: Tales of Race, Sex, and Hair*, ed. L. Jones and A. Rogers, 53–66. New York: Anchor.

Justice, D. H. 2004. "Seeing (Reading) Red: Indian Outlaws in the Ivory Tower." In *Indigenizing the Academy: Transforming and Empowering Communities*, ed. A. Mihesuah and A. C. Wilson, 100–123. Lincoln: University of Nebraska Press.

Katz, W. L. 1986. *Black Indians: A Hidden Heritage*. New York: Atheneum.

Ladson-Billings, G. 1999. "Just What Is Critical Race Theory, and What's It Doing in a *Nice* Field Like Education?" In *Race Is . . . Isn't: Critical Race Theory Qualitative Studies in Education*, ed. L. Parker, D. Deyhle, and S. Villenas, 7–30. Boulder, CO: Westview.

Lawrence, C. A. 1987. "The Id, the Ego, and Equal Protection: Reckoning with Unconscious Racism." *Stanford Law Review* 39 (2): 317–88.

Lawrence, C. A. 1995. "Racelessness." In *American Mixed Race: The Culture of Micro-diversity*, ed. N. Zack, 25–38. London: Rowman & Littlefield.

Lee, S. J. 2005. *Up against Whiteness: Race, School, and Immigrant Youth*. New York: Teachers College Press.

Leonardo, Z. 2002. "The Souls of White Folks: Critical Pedagogy, Whiteness Studies, and Globalization Discourse." *Race, Ethnicity and Education* 5 (1): 29–50. http://dx.doi.org/10.1080/13613320120117180.

Leonardo, Z. 2005. "The Color of Supremacy: Beyond the Discourse of 'White Privilege.'" In *Critical Pedagogy and Race*, ed. Z. Leonardo, 37–52. Malden, MA: Blackwell.

Lewis, A. 2003. "Some Are More Equal Than Others: Lessons on Whiteness from School." In *White Out: The Continuing Significance of Racism*, ed. A. Doane and E. Bonilla-Silva, 159–72. New York: Routledge.

Lewis, A. E. 2005. *Race in the Schoolyard: Negotiating the Color Line in Classrooms and Communities*. Piscataway, NJ: Rutgers University Press.

Lopez, A. M. 2001. "Measuring Race/Ethnicity: Identification Experiences of Mixed-Race and Multiethnic High School Students." PhD diss., University of California, Los Angeles.

Lopez, N. 2003. *Hopeful Girls, Troubled Boys*. New York: Routledge.

Lyda, J. 2008. "The Relationship between Multiracial Identity Variance, Social Connectedness, Facilitative Support, and Adjustment in Multiracial College Students." PhD diss., University of Oregon.

Makalani, M. 2001. "A Biracial Identity or a New Race? The Historical Limitations and Political Implications of a Biracial Identity." *Souls* 3 (4): 84.

Marez, C. 2001. "Signifying Spain, Becoming Comanche, Making Mexican: Indian Captivity and the History of Chicano/a Popular Performance." *American Quarterly* 53 (2): 267–307. http://dx.doi.org/10.1353/aq.2001.0018.

McQueen, N. 2002. "Racially and/or Culturally Mixed Individuals: How Does Education Influence the Cultural Identity of These Individuals and Conversely How Does Their Cultural Identity Influence Their Schooling?" MA thesis, University of Toronto.

Mihesuah, J. K. 2004. "Graduating Indigenous Students by Confronting the Academic Environment." In *Indigenizing the Academy: Transforming and Empowering Communities*, ed. A. Mihesuah and A. C. Wilson, 190–99. Lincoln: University of Nebraska Press.

Miller, R. L. 1992. "The Human Ecology of Multiracial Identity." In *Racially Mixed People in America*, ed. M. P. P. Root, 24–36. Newbury, CA: Sage.

Moore, T. 2006. "Mixed: Experiences of Biracial Students in an Urban High School." PhD diss., University of St. Thomas.

Morning, A. 2003. "New Faces, Old Faces: Counting the Multiracial Position." In *New Faces in a Changing America: Multiracial Identity in the 21st Century*, ed. L. Winters and H. DeBose, 41–67. Thousand Oaks, CA: Sage. http://dx.doi.org /10.4135/9781452233840.n3.

"Multiracials: Population." 2002. *American Demographics* 24 (10): S19.

Munoz-Miller, M. 2009. "Thinking outside the Box: Racial Self-identification Choice among Mixed Heritage Adolescents." PhD diss., University of Pennsylvania, Philadelphia.

Nieto-Phillips, J. M. 2004. *The Language of Blood: The Making of Spanish-American Identity in New Mexico*. Albuquerque: University of New Mexico Press.

Obama, B. 2008. "A More Perfect Union." Audio recording of a speech presented at the National Constitution Center, Philadelphia.

Omi, M., and H. Winant. 1986. *Racial Formation in the United States: From the 1960s to the 1980s*. London: Routledge.

Omi, M., and H. Winant. 1994. *Racial Formation in the United States from 1960s to 1990s*. New York: Routledge.

Phinney, J. S., and L. L. Alipuria. 1996. "At the Interface of Cultures: Multiethnic/ Multiracial High School and College Students." *Journal of Social Psychology* 136 (2): 139–58. http://dx.doi.org/10.1080/00224545.1996.9713988.

Potter, G. A. 2009. "The Invisibility of Multiracial Students: An Emerging Majority by 2050." PhD diss., San Diego State University.

Pulera, D. 2002. *Visible Differences: Why Race Will Matter to Americans in the Twenty-First Century*. New York: Continuum.

Renn, K. A. 1998. "Claiming Space: The College Experience of Biracial and Multiracial Students on Predominantly White Campuses." PhD diss., Boston College.

Roberts, D. 1997. *Killing the Black Body: Race, Reproduction, and the Meaning of Liberty*. New York: Pantheon.

Rockquemore, K. A., and D. L. Brunsma. 2002. *Beyond Black: Biracial Identity in America*. Thousand Oaks, CA: Sage.

Root, M. P. P. 1996. "A Bill of Rights for Racially Mixed People." In *The Multiracial Experience: Racial Borders as the New Frontier*, ed. M. P. P. Root, 3–14. Thousand Oaks, CA: Sage. http://dx.doi.org/10.4135/9781483327433.n1.

Root, M. P. P. 2001. *Love's Revolution: Interracial Marriage*. Philadelphia: Temple University Press.

Russell, K., M. Wilson, and R. Hall. 1992. *The Color Complex: The Politics of Skin Color among African Americans*. New York: Harcourt Brace Jovanovich.

Sanchez, C. E. 2004. "Communication Influences on Expression of Multiracial Identity in a Higher Education Context." PhD diss., University of New Mexico.

Snipp, C. M. 2002. "American Indians: Clues to the Future of Other Racial Groups." In *The New Race Question: How the Census Counts Multiracial Individuals*, ed. J. Perlmann and M. Waters, 189–214. New York: Russell Sage Foundations.

Soloranzo, D., and T. Yosso. 2002. "Critical Race Methogoloy: Counter-Storytelling as an Analytical Framework for Education Research." *Qualitative Inquiry* 8 (1): 23–44. http://dx.doi.org/10.1177/107780040200800103.

Spencer, R. 1997. "Race and Mixed Race: A Personal Tour." In *As We Are Now: Mixblood Essays on Race and Identity*, ed. W. S. Penn, 126–39. Berkeley: University of California Press.

Spencer, R. 1999. *Spurious Issues: Race and Multiracial Identity Politics in the United States*. Boulder, CO: Westview.

Spencer, R. 2006a. *Challenging Multiracial Identity*. Boulder, CO: Lynne Rienner.

Spencer, R. 2006b. "New Racial Identities, Old Arguments: Continuing Biological Reification." In *Mixed Messages: Multiracial Identities in the "Color-blind" Era*, ed. D. L. Brusma, 83–102. Boulder, CO: Lynne Rienner.

Spickard, P. R. 1989. *Mixed Blood: Intermarriage and Ethnic Identity in Twentieth-Century America*. Madison: University of Wisconsin Press.

Spivak, G. 1995. "Subaltern Studies: Deconstructing Historiography." In *The Spivak Reader: Selected Works by Gayatri Spivak*, ed. D. Landry and G. MacLeand, 203–36. New York: Routledge.

Stonequist, E. V. 1937. *The Marginal Man: A Study in Personality and Culture Conflict*. New York: Russell & Russell.

Storrs, D. 1996. "Mixed Race Women: The Construction and Contestation of Racial Boundaries, Meanings, and Identities." PhD diss., University of Oregon.

Stubblefield, A. 2001. "Racial Identity and Non-essentialism about Race." *Social Theory and Practice* 21:341–68.

Tatum, B. D. 1997. *Why Are All the Black Kids Sitting Together in the Cafeteria? And Other Conversations about Race*. New York: BasicBooks.

Taylor, E. 1998. "A Primer on Critical Race Theory." *Journal of Blacks in Higher Education* 19:122–24.

Texeira, M. T. 2003. "The New Multiracialism: An Affirmation of or an End to Race as We Know It?" In *New Faces in Changing America: Multiracial Identity in the 21st*

*Century*, ed. L. Winters and H. DeBose, 21–38. Thousand Oaks, CA: Sage. http://dx.doi.org/10.4135/9781452233840.n2.

Thompson, D. E. 2005. "Only Skin Deep? Identity and the Constitution of the Mixed-Race Subject." MA thesis, Carleton University.

Thompson, M. S., and V. M. Keith. 2001. "The Blacker the Berry: Gender, Skin Tone, Self-Esteem, and Self-Efficacy." *Gender and Society* 15 (3): 336–57. http://dx.doi.org/10.1177/089124301015003002.

Thorton, M. C. 1992. "Is Multiracial Status Unique? The Personal and Social Experience." In *Racially Mixed People in America*, ed. M. P. P. Root, 321–25. Newbury Park, CA: Sage.

US Census Bureau. 2000. "America Families and Living Arrangements: March 2000, and Earlier Reports." *Current Population Reports, series P-28: Special Censuses*:20–537.

Wijeyesinghe, C. 1992. "Towards an Understanding of the Racial Identity of Biracial People: The Experience of Racial Self-Identification of African-American/Euro-American Adults and the Factors Affecting Their Choices of Racial Identity." PhD diss., University of Massachusetts.

Williams, K. M. 2006. *Mark One or More: Civil Rights in Multiracial America*. Ann Arbor: University of Michigan Press. http://dx.doi.org/10.3998/mpub.17441.

Williams, T. K. 1992. "Prism Lives: Identity of Binational Americans." In *Racially Mixed People in America*, ed. M. P. P. Root, 280–303. Newbury Park, CA: Sage.

Williamson, J. 1995. *New People: Miscegenation and Mulattoes in the United States*. Baton Rouge: Louisiana State University Press.

Winters, L., and H. DeBose, eds. 2003. *New Faces in a Changing America: Multiracial Identity in the 21st Century*. Thousand Oaks, CA: Sage.

Wright, W. 1994. "One Drop of Blood." *New Yorker,* July 25, 46–55.

Zack, N. 1995. "Life After Race." In *American Mixed Race: The Culture of Microdiversity*, ed. N. Zack, 297–308. London: Rowman & Littlefield.

# Index

Made in United States
North Haven, CT
11 November 2024

60156257R00100